Ninety-Eight Years, Eleven Months, Nineteen Days

A Memoir

Vernon Devers

with

Elizabeth Ann Atkins

For information about this title or to order other books and/or electronic media, contact the publisher:

Two Sisters Writing & Publishing®
TwoSistersWriting.com
18530 Mack Avenue, Suite 166
Grosse Pointe Farms, MI 48236

ISBN   978-1-956879-34-6 (Hardcover)
ISBN   978-1-956879-35-3 (Paperback)
ISBN   978-1-956879-36-0 (eBook)

Printed in the United States of America

All the stories in this work are true.

Cover and Graphic Design: Illumination Graphics.
Author photos: The Devers Family Collection.

WHAT PEOPLE ARE SAYING ABOUT VERNON DEVERS

"While reading Vernon's chronology of his father's life, *Ninety-Eight Years, Eleven Months, Nineteen Days*, I noted his description of 'Dad.' He provides an account of the life of the man who nurtured him and his siblings and provided for his family, his 'Dad.'

There are many definitions and differences in defining a father versus a dad. A father can be anyone who sires a child, whereas a dad is the man who gives his love and strength to his family and provides guidance for their well-being.

Vernon shares memories growing up and how 'Dad' shaped his life and that of his brothers and sisters. 'PAPA D's' love did not stop with his children. His life was full of stories from family members about 'Uncle D,' who shared his love through his actions and deeds with his siblings, children, and extended family helping them to grow and flourish.

Vernon captures significant notes during the life of his dad that will give others examples on how to be a 'Dad.' Every family should have a 'Dad' like 'PAPA D.' His character, faith, and wisdom gave his family a strong and lasting foundation.

For those who read *Ninety-Eight Years, Eleven Months, Nineteen Days*, you will find inspiration and guidance on family, devotion, and love through the life of Albany Devers."

— **Henry L. Green, Hon. AIA**
Former President, National Institute of Building Sciences

"This book is a truly pleasurable read about a black family thriving in the South in the 20th century. It is a story about the strength and endurance of the family and its patriarch who through love, faith and resilience, weathered so many challenges and changes over an amazing century of life. It illustrates so beautifully how a family of modest means and limited opportunities from any race, creed or religion can flourish and grow by following the example of a life lived with courage, dignity and simple unshakeable values."

— **Kathleen Lopilato, JD, CPCU**
VICE PRESIDENT
HOME OFFICE LEGAL
Auto-Owners Insurance

"This book is not only a tribute to a father's life, but demonstrates how a Black patriarch leads and keeps his family intact during segregation in Louisiana with determination and faith. Many historical and life lessons can be learned by anyone who reads about D's life. Highly recommend reading for all!"

— **Metodi Pogoncheff, D.D.S., P.C.**

Dedication

This book is dedicated to fathers and mothers, young
and old, to adults of all ages, to teenagers, to children,
to educators, and to all others who have the desire
to learn things from a wonderful Dad.

Foreword

When first contacted by Vernon regarding his book project, I have to say I was surprised. Not because he actually did write his book, which yes, is a bit surprising—lots of people say they are going to write books and never do. But also because he did it so well, with so much feeling, it was a side of Vernon I really didn't know, but was pleased to learn about while reading about his dad.

I had worked with Vernon for his entire career. I knew him to be quiet, yet conscientious. Thorough in his work, and good in what he did, but private about his personal life. I don't ever recall him talking about his father or his feelings for him, or his family. So to share this story of the life of the man that I now see Vernon himself is so much alike, opened an inside story of someone I might have known after working together for 36 years. After reading the book, I got a closer look and a better understanding of Vernon, his work, his family and his life, and of course the influence behind Vernon's own life.

Further intriguing me about his project was my own relationship with my father. Unlike Vernon's father, my dad passed on far too soon. He's been gone almost 50 years, departing due to cancer while I was a freshman in college. He was to me what "D," or "Uncle D" was to Vernon and his family. He was my rock, my mentor, often my inspiration. Reading this book brought my own thoughts, memories, and stories of my dad, back to life for me. As I went through life, a thought I often shared was, *I hope my dad would have been proud of me.* I sense this same sentiment from the pages of this book, and readily say, "Vernon, your dad would be very proud of you! It is obvious you were proud of him." I enjoyed the memories the book shared, the memories this book triggered, and am grateful for you sharing his, and your story.

— **Jeffrey F. Harrold**
Former Chairman and CEO, Auto-Owners
Insurance Company

Contents

Acknowledgments

It is with great pleasure that I thank my wife Sheila for listening to me as I told her I would write this book. I thank her for proofreading my work and all of her support and love. My years of employment helped me discover and develop some writing skills, and for this, I am truly thankful.

I thank my brother, Albany S., for shining some light about his recall of our dad. He is Dad's first son and I am Dad's last son and child. Dad was wonderful to all of his children. I thank Albany for his valuable support as I worked on writing this book about our dad.

My first cousins, Laverne Flanagan, Charles Devers, Oscar Devers, and Josephine Brewster, spent more than 60 years of their lives with their dear Uncle D. Their comments about Dad are very much appreciated.

Our two children, Jeremy and Jerran, when asked to share a comment or two about their experiences with Dad, readily jumped at the opportunity. I am very grateful for their love and support.

To my brother-in-law, Leon Green, thank you for your help with pictures and your overall support.

I am grateful for the directions, encouragement, and kind, positive words of my most valuable publisher, Elizabeth Ann Atkins, co-creator of Two Sisters Writing & Publishing®. Thank you for your great help!

All of you helped make my writing this book a pleasure.

A Special Thank You

When Dad was no longer able to care for himself and his second wife, Doris, my brother Albert and his wife, Earsel, stepped up to assist Dad and Doris. They helped them to remain in Dad's house for the last several years of Dad's life. Albert and Earsel provided all forms of daily care for Dad and Doris. Their care was appreciated by Dad and Doris. When my family and I visited Dad and Doris, we saw firsthand their tireless efforts. All the while Albert was helping with the care, he was battling cancer. At the writing of this book, I am pleased to say that Albert is now 75 years old and he is doing fine.

Thank you, brother and sister-in-law.

Introduction

For the grandchildren, great-grandchildren, and great-great-grandchildren who did not have the pleasure or opportunity to spend much time with or to know Dad, it is my hope that the following content will give you some glimpse into who Dad was and that you appreciate his legacy.

Perhaps you only received a hug! Or sat momentarily on his lap! Or saw him sitting in a chair! Whatever memories you have of him, say, "Thank you," as many others never get to see a granddad, let alone a great- or great-great-granddad.

You can be assured that your visit with Dad always left him with much to reflect upon for a long time. For years, I wondered:

Will Dad live to be 100 years old? Will he stay healthy as he aged? Will any of his children live to equal or exceed his age?

As the years have come and gone, some of the questions have been answered. Yes, Dad stayed healthy as he aged. He required few daily prescriptions up to his death.

During my father Albany Devers' lifetime from 1917 until 2016, the following are some Notable, Significant, and Game-Changing historic events that may have been most important to Dad.

Notable Things

1. *The Star-Spangled Banner* was adopted as the national anthem in 1931.
2. The Fair Labor Standard Act established the first minimum wage in the United States at 25 cents per hour in 1938.
3. The United States declared war on Japan on December 7, 1941.
4. Dr. Martin Luther King, Jr. delivered his "I Have a Dream" speech in 1963.
5. The First Super Bowl was played in 1967.
6. Sandra Day O'Connor was sworn in as the first woman Supreme Court Justice in 1981.

Significant Things

1. The Vietnam War raged from 1955 until 1975.
2. President John F. Kennedy was assassinated on November 22, 1963.
3. Segregation legally ended with the passing of the Civil Rights Act of 1964.

4. Dr. Martin Luther King, Jr. was assassinated on April 4, 1968.
5. Humans landed on the moon in 1969.
6. The World Trade Center terrorist attacks happened on September 11, 2001.
7. Barack Obama was sworn in as President of the United States in 2009.

Game-Changing Things

1. The Spanish Flu global pandemic claimed millions of lives in 1918.
2. The Great Depression occurred between 1929 and 1939.
3. Social Security began in 1935.
4. The United States was victorious in defeating fascism with World War I and World War II.
5. Jackie Robinson was the first Black person to play in Major League Baseball in 1947.

Dad and Mom, who did not subscribe to any newspaper, loved to watch the evening news, where they learned of these historic events. Back in the 1950s and 1960s, people wholeheartedly trusted what the newscaster reported. In fact, a poll showed that Walter Cronkite, anchor of *The CBS Evening News,* was considered "the most trusted man in America."

When other adults visited with Dad and Mom, I loved listening to their conversations. I was not eavesdropping; I was merely within listening distance.

I recall the sadness on Dad's and Mom's faces over the assassinations of President John F. Kennedy and Dr. Martin Luther King, Jr. JFK was the hope of a better life for many Black people. His death was like letting the air out of a balloon, deflating the vision for justice, equality, and economic empowerment. Neither of my parents would speak to me as a youth about these events, as many adults did not talk to their children about real, hard-hitting issues and events during that era.

The assassination of Dr. Martin Luther King, Jr. further saddened my parents. Dr. King was the leader of the Black people. His death scared my parents and they cautioned me to watch what I would say and do, to keep from getting into trouble and hurt or killed.

The assassinations of JFK and Dr. King, and many other historic events, helped mold my parents' thinking, actions and decisions. Their lives were impacted for both good and bad, and contributed to how they raised my siblings and me.

Dad lived for 98 years, 11 months and 19 days. He was born on February 1, 1917, in Greenwood, Louisiana. Greenwood is in Caddo Parish, which is located in the northwest corner of Louisiana, bordering Texas to the west and Arkansas to the north. He had four brothers and three sisters:

• Samuel Devers, Jr. was born in 1905 and died in 1956.

• Lola (Devers) Smith was born on September 15, 1906, and died on July 18, 2004.

• Curtis Devers was born in 1908 and died in 2001.

· Ola (Devers) Long was born in 1911 and died in 1985.

· Ernest Devers was born on April 19, 1913, and died on February 23, 2001.

· Nathaniel Devers was born in 1915 and died in 2002.

· Daisy (Devers) Richardson was born on January 30, 1920, and died on April 30, 2013.

My father died on January 20, 2016, in Shreveport, Louisiana, and is buried in Northwest Louisiana Veterans Cemetery in Keithville, Louisiana.

This book is about his long, healthy and contented life. After marrying twice, raising six children, working and retiring, and cultivating a home that was abundant with good food, family fun and faith, he became an old man, enjoying a simple life while providing so many good examples for people to learn from and apply every day.

Dad was called by various names. Some people called him "Uncle D"; others called him "Shorty"; still others called him "D Duck"; "PAPA D"; and lastly, almost all called him "D." I knew him by all these names.

Now, for you and all others, here is a glimpse of my dad.

— **Vernon Devers**

Chapter 1 — Family

⁂

*W*hen my father, Albany Devers, was born in Greenwood, Louisiana on February 1, 1917, World War I was raging while life in the segregated American South relegated most Colored people to difficult and dangerous circumstances that included impoverished, back-breaking work as sharecroppers.

While few details are known about the circumstances of my father's early years, he grew up in a family rooted in love, faith, land ownership and education that provided a strong foundation to live and thrive for nearly a century.

His parents, Samuel and Lessie Devers, were land-owners who instilled in him the mental fortitude and Christian values required to survive during an era that was especially threatening for Colored boys and men.

His father Samuel was born around 1878 and his mother Lessie came into the world about a year later. They lived on 120 acres of land that our family owned on U.S. Highway 80 in Greenwood, Louisiana, a small town in Caddo Parish in the northwest corner of the state bordering Texas and Arkansas.

Since the 1850s, Greenwood had flourished with 100 wagons, pulled by eight or 10 oxen each, passing through the town every day as people patronized seven stores, a 15-room hotel, nine saloons, a Masonic Lodge, two two-story schools, a Methodist church, five physicians, and businesses that included three brick yards, a wagon and plow factory, a foundry and machine shop, a tan yard, a saddlery, a distillery, a blacksmith shop and a tin shop.[1]

My grandparents were born less than two decades after President Abraham Lincoln signed the Emancipation Proclamation on January 1, 1863, during the third year of the Civil War, freeing all people who had been enslaved. That freedom was slow to take effect, and while few details are known about my grandparents' work and daily lives during that time, Samuel and Lessie married on December 17, 1902.

"The Old Home Place was the house where Grandpa Sam and Grandma Lessie got married," said my cousin, Oscar Devers, during an interview for this book. Now 81, he lives on Devers Road in Greenwood on property owned by our family for several generations.

"They built the house and married in 1902," Cousin Oscar said.

In that home, Grandpa Sam and Grandma Lessie enjoyed a 45-year marriage that brought eight children into the world. Their children were: Samuel Devers, Jr. in 1905; Lola

Devers in 1906; Curtis Devers in 1908; Ola Devers in 1911; Ernest Devers in 1913; Nathaniel Devers in 1915; my father, Albany Devers, in 1917; and Daisy Devers in 1920.

My oldest brother, Albany Samuel, now a 79-year-old author living in Chicago, Illinois, spent many years researching and documenting Devers' family ancestry, visiting cemeteries in Louisiana and Texas, and conducting in-person interviews with elderly family members.

"I observed the deep sense of regret in my father and all of his siblings," Albany said. "They yearned for knowledge of their grandparents and generations before them, but they were void of information because their parents, Sam and Lessie, just like many other Black folks, didn't talk about the ills of slavery and segregation."

Dad grew up in Greenwood, Louisiana, which remains a small town of nine square miles with a population of 3,166 as of the 2020 U.S. Census.[2] It is located 15 miles west of downtown Shreveport.

With limited access to many commercial goods and services, Dad and his parents relied on living off the land, raising chickens, hogs and crops for sustenance. This hard work taught my father and his siblings many valuable life lessons, such as rising early and taking care of their animals and other possessions, so that they would produce and last a long time.

When he was a teenager, Dad wanted to follow in his older brothers' footsteps by serving in the U.S. Army. Years later, Dad achieved his wish by serving in the Army.

His rank was TEC 5. That rank was given to noncombat soldiers who had special technical skills between 1942 and 1948. Dad's skill was cooking, as he was a cook in the Army while based in Alabama.

When Dad was 24, he married 18-year-old Luella Hunter, who was born on February 22, 1923, in Waskom, Texas, a small town at the Louisiana state line known as "the gateway to Texas." Waskom is located on the Interstate 20 highway, a major east-west route.

Married on July 20, 1941, they were a beautiful couple. Dad was 5'10" and thin. Mom was 5'2"—not fat, not skinny. They celebrated the births of six children:

1. Sylvia Moch was born on March 8, 1942. She died on August 13, 2013. She was 71.

2. Albany Samuel Devers was born on January 1, 1944. He is not a junior (because our father did not have a middle name) and did not like it when people called him that until adulthood, when he asked people to address him as Albany. He is 79.

3. Raymond was born on November 2, 1945. He died on April 4, 2014. He was 68.

4. Albert Devers was born on November 11, 1947. He is 75.

5. Patricia Green was born on July 24, 1949. She died on March 16, 2018. She was 68.

6. Vernon Devers (me) was born on October 28, 1952. I am 70 years old.

My sister Sylvia was born while Dad was serving in the military.

Cousin Oscar recalled when Uncle D was discharged from the Army and returned home. "I'll never forget," Cousin Oscar said, "he got off the bus and said, 'Here!' and gave me a little tobacco sack. Years ago, they sold cigarette tobacco in a little cloth bag where you roll your own cigarettes because everybody couldn't afford to buy rolled cigarettes. I'll never forget, he gave me a bag of pennies. Those pennies might still be stuck here somewhere."

Cousin Charles, now 85 years old, recalled that after the military, Uncle D worked at a sawmill for a while and he built a house. He worked with the carpenter at the sawmill to learn some of the trade skills. Later, Uncle D hired the carpenter to build his house on Rockwell Place.

In 1952, when I was born as the youngest child, we lived in an extended family compound of homes on about 120 acres of land in Greenwood near the Louisiana-Texas border. This was the same land where my father's parents had built their home in 1902 or 1903, and it was known as "The Old Home Place," according to Cousin Oscar. Living amongst aunts, uncles and cousins made life very enjoyable, pleasant and secure for us all.

First cousin, Josephine Brewster, a daughter of Dad's brother Ernest, is a retired paralegal who lives in Dallas.

She recalled all of us—aunts, uncles, and cousins—being very close and family-oriented. As children and first cousins, we were always together. We played together. We loved just being around each other for the fellowship and the fun.

She remembered that, "Uncle D had such a contagious smile. My Uncle D smoked cigars. I don't know if it was lit or if he just had it in his mouth. That was part of his persona; it was his signature. He was fun-loving and had lots of jokes. He was a Christian, Godly man."

My brother Albany added, "His generation was deeply entrenched in the extended family. They shared almost everything, from children, animals, food crops, money and more. If some family member didn't have money for clothing, that person was provided for without question. Food was never a concern, because they lived off land owned by them."

This lifestyle and core value enabled Dad to honor his mother, Grandma Lessie, who was the matriarch of our family. She lived with Aunt Daisy and her husband, Uncle Eddie. Beside them lived Uncle Buddy (Ernest Senior) and his wife, Aunt Viola, and their nine children who included my cousins Josephine, Oscar and Charles.

On the other side was our house, so Grandma Lessie had two sons and a daughter living around her. We all loved and cared for her and for one another. As for Grandma Lessie's other children, Uncle Curtis lived in Houston, Uncle Nathaniel and Aunt Ola lived in California, and Aunt Lola lived in Shreveport.

Though I never met my grandfather, who died at age 69 in 1947, five years before my birth, I was privileged to live around my grandmother for 17 years. Grandma Lessie was forgetful of her grandchildren's names.

"Whose child are you?" she often asked us.

Us grandchildren would laugh. In a spirit of playful love, my sister, Pat, and cousin, Josephine, would sneak and hide Grandma Lessie's cane.

"Where's my cane?" Grandma Lessie would ask, making the girls giggle.

Dad and his siblings greatly respected Grandma Lessie. She never had to worry about love and care as she grew older. She died at age 91 on April 27, 1971.

Except for his two years serving in the Army, Dad spent more than 50 years living around his mom. They had a very good relationship. My relationship with Grandma Lessie was also very good. The living arrangement of our extended family was evidence of Dad and his siblings having been raised to be respectful and kind to older family members. It also resulted in Dad having good relationships with his sisters, then with his first wife (my mom), then with his daughters and later with his second wife (Doris). He set the example for his sons and others to have and show respect for females and to create good, long-standing relationships. This core value has been passed down by each generation of our family.

My parents, aunts and uncles also emphasized the importance of education to guarantee success in life. My mother attended public schools in Waskom, Texas, but did not graduate from high school. For the first three or four years of my life, she was a maid at a hotel in Shreveport and a nursing aide, having received her training at Caddo Community Center.

INTERSTATE 20 LEADS US TO OUR NEW HOME

In the early 1950s, the federal government announced the birth of the Interstate Highway System. When Interstate 20 was constructed, it cut straight through our family's property. The government purchased the land from our family, and we all moved to different homes.

My parents moved us closer to Shreveport. They purchased two lots in a new subdivision in the country, and hired a Black contractor, Mr. Lee, to build our ranch-style home. We were the only house on the west side of Rockwell Place, a paved street.

Our white house with black trim had three bedrooms, a family room/den, a combination dining and living room, a kitchen and one bathroom. We had no basement or garage, but we did have a carport with a storage area that housed a large, deep freezer where we kept food for the wintertime.

Summertime in Shreveport is humid, with temperatures in the mid-90s in July and August. We tried to cool the house by opening the windows or using a fan. When I was a teenager, my parents purchased a window air conditioner and installed it in the dining/living room. They added a second one in a bedroom.

The bathroom was very hot and lacked an exhaust fan. We also did not have a shower—just a bathtub. After a bath, it was very difficult to dry off. You would keep sweating as you wiped with a towel. Still, we endured the discomfort.

Our parents had the coolest room in the house because their bedroom was in the southwest corner and our house faced east. My two sisters shared a bedroom and us four boys shared one large bed in another room. When Albany was 16, he went to live with Aunt Lola in downtown Shreveport, leaving me with Albert and Raymond to share our room.

THE GRASS & THE GARDEN

The grass on the attached lots would grow into weeds, so we'd cut beyond our lots to create more space and stop critters from dwelling near us. Our yard had St. Augustine grass. It was always thick and green and we did not water it. The morning dew apparently was enough moisture. I do not recall us ever fertilizing the lawn. Dad loved mowing it and so did I. When I became strong enough to start the mower, I could not wait to get home from school and start mowing. I wanted to be working and getting as much done as possible before Dad arrived home from work. I enjoyed it very much. Imagine, it is 3:00 PM, hot and humid, there I am mowing the grass in a long-sleeved shirt.

The subdivision bordered property owned by Mr. Thomas, who gave us permission to use as much of the land as we wanted to build a garden. So, my parents cleared out a large section in the back and cultivated a large garden. Mr. Thomas loaned Dad his mule and a plow. Dad did the labor-intensive work of standing behind the plow as the mule pulled it to prepare the dirt for planting.

Starting in March, weather permitting due to frequent rains, we always planted a robust garden that grew until fall. In front of the garden, we had strawberry plants. Mom and Dad also planted some pecan trees, a peach tree, some plum trees and a pear tree. I loved eating the large plums in the spring and collecting brown grocery bags full of pecans in the fall.

My parents, who grew up in agricultural environments, loved to garden together. I was not as enthused about working in the garden, because it involved weeding with a hoe and I was always afraid, wondering, *What if there's a snake?* Guess what? One day as I dug in the ground in the garden, I came upon a large, light and dark brown snake. It was a *loooong* time before I went back into the garden.

Our garden produced abundant harvests that we ate as the crops matured and froze the rest for the winter. In addition to fresh vegetables in the freezer, we had plenty of beef and pork, as well as fresh fish caught from local ponds.

The beef came from cows on property in Texas that Mom inherited from her mother. The property had oil and gas on it, and my mom and grandmother had signed contracts with oil and gas companies, granting them the right to drill; those companies sent royalty payments to Mom throughout the year. That income, along with Dad's income, helped us buy the things we needed. We always had enough to eat, freeze and give away.

We had six or seven cows on the Texas property. Every year, Dad slaughtered a cow and filled the deep freezer with beef. Dad gave some away, and we traded some with a cousin who had a hog farm. Every year, Cousin Thomas slaughtered some, so we traded beef for pork that filled our freezer. We bought chicken from the store. As for fish, my parents loved fishing in the local ponds in the woods around Louisiana. They left early in the morning, sat quietly on the bank, cast their lines, and waited for fish to bite. Excellent tasting was that fish! I tried fishing with them, but lacked the patience to just sit there waiting for the fish to bite.

Dad also went squirrel hunting, something he had enjoyed since childhood. None of us had any interest in doing that or eating squirrel meat. So, when he brought it home, he gave it away.

My cousin, Oscar Devers, who is 11 years older than me and the son of Dad's brother, Ernest, and his wife, Aunt Viola, remembers outings with Dad, whom he said was like a big brother.

"Uncle D would always take his oldest boy and girl and come get me," Oscar said. "He'd say, 'C'mon, boy, let's go ride.' And we'd go visit The Old Home Place and on into East Texas."

Oscar, a retired U.S. Army reservist who worked for General Electric, remembered how Dad was known for keeping an unlit cigar in his mouth.

"He didn't ever smoke the cigar; he just kept it in his mouth," Oscar said. "Uncle D was sort of like a maverick. He kept him a little bottle in his pocket. He nipped off of it. It was a half pint or pint of Seagram's 7 whiskey, and he kept it in his car."

Oscar said Dad and our uncles hunted together.

"They would go hunting every Friday to get food to eat," Oscar said during an interview for this book. "The uncles would come back with bags and go out in the yard and dump all that meat out and divvy it up right there— raccoons, possums, squirrels, armadillos. Every Friday, the women would cook the food."

Let me be clear, I never ate any raccoon, possum, squirrel or armadillo.

With nine kids (in Uncle Buddy and Aunt Viola's home), Oscar said the food didn't last long. "To store the uncooked meats," he added, "we kept them cold in the ice box with blocks of ice that were delivered every two or three days by the ice man. Uncle D was one of the first ones to get a refrigerator, so we kept some meats in his refrigerator to keep them from spoiling."

ENJOYING MOM'S HOMECOOKED MEALS

Mom rose before dawn every workday, Monday through Friday and some Saturdays when Dad worked. She didn't have an alarm and instead relied on her internal body clock. If you told her, "I need to get up at 3 AM," then she could wake up and get you up at 3 AM. Every morning, wearing a dress and never pants, she headed to the kitchen, which had a gas stove, refrigerator, double sinks, brown walnut cabinets, a small counter space and a linoleum floor.

Mom's morning meals filled the house with the scents of homemade biscuits, bacon, sausage and eggs that Dad enjoyed before work. The rest of us—for several years, all six of us brothers and sisters lived at home—got up later and ate the same breakfast. We all loved grape jelly on the biscuits. We also had heavy syrup, the Brer Rabbit brand. I wanted my parents to buy different types of syrup, but they never did.

When we were raising chickens, we ate fresh brown eggs. I felt like we were country folks. I wanted my parents to buy white eggs from the store, like other families did. That was unsettling to me. I wondered, *Why do we have to eat those brown eggs? Why can't we eat store-bought eggs?* Guess what eggs my wife and I eat today? Brown eggs.

In the morning, Mom also packed Dad's lunch that he took to his physically strenuous job at the local Ralston Purina factory in Shreveport, making feed for animals. To sustain his energy, she packed him heavy comfort foods such as fried chicken, bread and peas—often leftovers from the previous night's dinner. Dad never complained about what she prepared for breakfast, lunch or dinner.

Dad never talked to me about his place of employment, his work or any of his workplace associates. I merely saw him get up early, clean up, eat breakfast and go off to work. He would return home later in the afternoon or evening.

Dad worked while Mom stayed home, cared for household affairs and helped raise us children. Dad never used verbal or physical punishment with me. To my knowledge, Dad never was abusive to anyone. I also never heard my parents argue or be angry with each other. Likewise, I never saw them hugging or kissing.

We lived modestly. We never had way too much or too little. My parents knew how to stretch their money to make it go far.

In the middle of the day, my mother started preparing for dinner. We ate all kinds of peas: black-eyed peas, purple hull peas, crowder peas, green peas—all fresh and all grown in our garden or obtained from another farmer. The scent wafted throughout the house and was wonderful.

Mom prepared fresh foods from the garden: corn; mustard, turnip and collard greens; okra; carrots; white and sweet potatoes; tomatoes; cucumbers; watermelon; cantaloupe; strawberries; and green beans. We also ate

Cushaw squash, a delicacy. Mealtime included a lot of rice as well as rolls and cornbread.

Meat was usually fried chicken, pork chops, liver and fish. Dad loved to barbecue chicken, pork chops and ribs.

"Ooooooh, Uncle D could barbecue!" Oscar exclaimed. "I never cared too much for it, but oooh, he could barbecue! Yes, indeed! Wooo! My wife (Val Marie) would jump off the Empire State Building to get some barbecue. Uncle D also had a garden with peas and corn. He could raise the best garden. He was attentive to little old small stuff like most people forgot. He could cook inside or out."

Dad also prepared briskets for Aunt Daisy because she loved them.

We drank water, Kool-Aid, pop and RC Royal Crown Cola. Dad didn't drink alcohol around us and Mom only used it when she baked fruit cakes.

At mealtime, even for Sunday dinner, we all prepared our plates in the kitchen, where our parents sat to eat at the table that had three or four chairs. Us kids took our plates outside to eat on the carport, or go into the den to watch TV, usually the news or a sports game.

We had a living room-dining room area with a China cabinet and table, but we hardly ever ate in there.

We were all hungry and we ate to our delight. There were no complaints, just full and satisfied stomachs. After dinner, Dad would go outside, sit in one of the comfortable chairs, put his cigar in his mouth. Yes, and he lit it! He took a few puffs and let the cigar extinguish itself. He was at peace and relaxed. Many days, he, Mom and I would just sit on the carport, say a few words, but mostly look around in silence.

Dad and Mom were very pleased with the home life they were providing for the family. Dad worked to earn money, Mom worked at caring for and helping to maintain our home. I learned how to be a family and how to take care of possessions and enjoy each day from my parents and their examples.

Security is what Dad and Mom provided for us.

INSTILLED WITH STRONG VALUES

My brother Albany is grateful for how our parents instilled good values in us and always supported our goals.

"As a little boy," Albany said, "I wanted to be like Matt Dillon with a big pistol on my side. 'No pistol,' Dad said. I wanted to play the trumpet like Louie Armstrong, so he bought me a trumpet. He wanted me to play baseball, but I wanted nothing to do with baseball, so he didn't force me. Instead, he focused his baseball desires in the direction of my brothers Raymond and Albert. Raymond wanted nothing to do with baseball; he preferred spending his time practicing the drums, so Dad picked on the little guy, Albert, because he was eager to stand up to his challenge. Dad showed no mercy on poor Albert and treated the little fella as his equal. A short time later, Albert wanted nothing to do with baseball. He was washed up in less than a week. He now wanted to play the tenor saxophone like John Coltrane."

Albany continued, "You see, baseball was Dad's thing because he came up in the day of the Negro Baseball League. It was almost sacrosanct for boys in his day not to play baseball."

Albany also expressed tremendous respect for our mother.

"The most impactful person in my life was my mother," Albany said. "I respected her as my mother, but in reality, she was one of my closest friends. Dad was not my friend. He was my father. For example, whenever I became too big for my breeches, Mama would say, 'Wait until your daddy gets home. He will tan your behind.' Nothing else needed to be said. I behaved like an angel for the rest of the day."

Lastly, Albany added, "*Do unto others as you would have them do unto you*, was not just something quoted from biblical scripture; it was taught and strongly enforced while growing up in my father's house."

MOM'S QUILTS KEPT US WARM

When she wasn't cooking or cleaning or gardening, Mom enjoyed watching a soap opera on TV. She also spent a lot of time sitting on the carport, making the heavy quilts that kept us warm when the nighttime temperatures dipped to 20 degrees from October, when we started wearing winter coats, until February. It rarely snowed, and one time when it did, our school was immediately closed. Our house did not have central heating, but we were never cold under Mom's homemade quilts.

She sewed them with the help of two wooden "horses," which Dad built with one board across and one board down, and legs to stabilize them. She then secured the growing quilt over the horses, constantly moving them as the quilt expanded on her bookend-type workspace. It was fascinating to watch her sit there using the needle, thread and thimble, connecting two layers of cotton and/ or wool fabric over the interior batting to create a big, thick, heavy quilt, using pieces of cloth that folks gave to her. Mom was very talented, but her skills were not passed down to the next generation because my sisters did not want to learn how to make quilts.

Each of us had a quilt; mine had stars and stripes. Those quilts were incredibly warm after we turned off the little gas heaters in each bedroom before going to sleep. The heaters kept the whole house warm. They required turning on a pilot, then a parent or older sibling would use a match to light the gas coming out to turn on the gas heater. For safety, we turned them off while we slept. In the morning, the heaters were lit again to warm the kitchen and den.

CHURCH TEACHES IMPORTANT LESSONS

Every Sunday, Dad and our family got into Dad's pea-green, two-door 1955 Chevrolet Belle Air, which he had purchased brand new. He drove us 10 miles to attend services at Union Chapel Missionary Baptist Church in Waskom, Texas, where Mom was born and raised.

All the family—including Dad's brother Ernest, Aunt Viola and their nine kids, and Dad's youngest sister Daisy and her husband Eddie—attended this church. The 70 congregants dressed up in suits and ties. My dress clothes included a suit and dress shoes.

Like the other women, Mom wore a hat and gloves. As a Pastor's Aide, she wore all white, as did the female ushers, and together they tended to people who were falling out with the Holy Spirit.

Dad served as a deacon and helped organize church events and operations. Sometimes he sat with the family; other times he was doing deacon duties and serving as president of the Usher Board. His brother Ernest, who was nicknamed Buddy, was the treasurer for about 60 years. When dementia developed, Dad replaced him as the treasurer.

As the treasurer, Dad brought money back to the house after the service. We had no security alarm and we did not have to worry about theft. On Monday, he went to the bank in Texas to deposit the money into the church's bank account. Dad served in that position until he grew old and was no longer able to perform the duties.

At our church, the congregants had diverse occupations and interacted with harmony. They ranged from low income to middle class. My dad's youngest sister Daisy was a college graduate and a schoolteacher, married to Uncle Eddie, a mortician who had earned a military medal for bravery. He worked for a funeral home that he would eventually own. They were middle class and couldn't have children. A number of people in the church were schoolteachers.

During the service, I was happy when the minister got the Holy Spirit and began to hum and got excited, and the organist began to insert some music during the sermon; this meant that service was almost over. Remember, I was a young person.

This led me to daydream and observe amusing moments such as the fact that the audience didn't know the words to the songs like "Amazing Grace." Rather than sing, the men would hum along with the music. Even today, if you ask me any gospel song, I don't know the words. Not one.

Likewise, I never heard my dad pray or read. In fact, I didn't know if he could read. Then, when I was older, my dad was reading something from the paper. It surprised me, and I thought, *He can read very well.*

I enjoyed going to church. I was always scared of going up into its small balcony because it felt spooky. We held a lot of funerals in the church and at that time, I was fearful of the dead. Other than that, the preaching and singing were fine. We never had someone who was an outstanding singer who lifted the roof during my upbringing.

Our church was organized in 1868 and its red brick building has stood all my life. When I was growing up, it did not have restrooms. There were outhouses with nowhere to clean your hands. They stunk badly. At times, there was no toilet paper. You learned to hold it until you arrived home. How did we stay healthy? Somehow, no communicable sickness occurred. What a blessing!

The church had no central air conditioning or heating. Many times, Dad and our family would arrive early in the fall and winter and he would use matches to light the church's gas heaters. I walked with him and watched. This was dangerous—turning on the gas and using a match to light the pilot gas. If it had blown up, there was no telling what may have happened. I was not mature at praying then, yet God must have known what I wanted to say, because no incident ever occurred. Those heaters warmed that building very well.

For a future history lesson, it would be interesting to learn the history of the actual construction of the current structure, which has a large auditorium and a wing behind it. Who designed the building? Where did the money come from to build the structure? Who were the workers performing the construction? How long did it take to build? I am sure some young reader of this book or some other person will bring answers to these questions and many more points to light.

Church taught us kids to be respectful, honest and truthful in dealings with people, and to be fair and friendly, loving and mannerly. It was not acceptable for a young person to call an adult by their first name;

it was considered disrespectful. (Many years later, my first cousin Laverne, who was in her sixties, took offense when my five-year-old son Jeremy called her by her first name.)

After church services, people fellowshipped outdoors. Dad was outgoing, friendly and talkative. Mom was more reserved, but could carry on a conversation. Us kids would talk with each other.

When it was time to drive home, we all piled into the front and back seats, sitting on each other's laps. Back then, the law did not require us to wear seatbelts. The front seat had no console, so we could squeeze into the middle. Since Uncle Buddy and Aunt Viola had nine kids, they made two trips to and from church.

During football season, I was always eager for the 11 AM service to end so we could get home to watch the football game at 1 PM. Since I loved the Dallas Cowboys, my family always let me have the TV.

At dinnertime, the minister sometimes came to our home for Sunday dinner or Mom took him a meal.

The Church was impactful for Dad and Mom, and they passed this way of life onto their children. Now some of us are living and passing this way of life onto the next generation.

AN INHERITANCE THAT DIDN'T HAPPEN

My mother's cousin, Roberta Ragland, and her husband, Will Ragland, wanted a child so badly, but they were older and unable to have children. When I was born, they saw me as the child they couldn't have.

"Can I hold him?" Cousin Roberta asked in church when I was an infant. My parents agreed.

Then they asked my parents, "Can we take him home with us and you pick him up later Sunday evening?" After that, they asked to have me spend all of Saturday with them, and they would bring me to church with them on Sunday. They kept asking for more and more time.

Cousin Will was a farmer and they lived deep in the country. No other houses were around. With no indoor plumbing or electricity, the house was lit by oil lamps and had no outdoor lights. It was scary out there.

My cousin Roberta worked six days a week as a maid for a white family in Waskom. On Saturdays, when I was with her, she took me with her to work and I played with their two daughters.

While I spent significant time with cousins Roberta and Will, my brother Albany did the same with other family members.

When I was six or seven, Cousin Will died. Cousin Roberta moved into Waskom and had a house built on land they owned. She died not long after Cousin Will.

They owned acres and acres that were rich with oil and gas. Because they had no heirs, Cousin Roberta had mentioned to Dad and Mom that they were going to leave everything to me. My dad was scared about having to manage their assets until I reached the age of 21, so he said no.

The property went to some other people.

"That was yours," my brother Albany told me.

If Dad had said yes, then my life would have developed a different way. I am happy how things turned out.

SEGREGATION AT SCHOOL, AT WORK AND IN THE COMMUNITY

We lived in the segregated South, where the law stated that Colored and white people had separate public accommodations. Much duplication existed: one for Colored, one for white.

This was especially true for schools. Rather than one elementary school, middle school and high school for all children, our town had separate schools for white kids and Black kids.

I rode the bus to attend all-Black schools where all my teachers except one were Black and had graduated from Historically Black Colleges and Universities (HBCUs) such as Grambling State University, Texas Southern University, Wiley College, and Bishop College. (In contrast, my wife Sheila had only two Black teachers at schools that she attended while growing up in the North.)

In the end, I believe that Dad's physical work at his job was a factor in his health and longevity. Over the years, the white men who worked in the offices died off, as did his Black co-workers. But Dad continued to live strong without medicine, without health problems, until he was 98.

Back in the 1950s and 1960s, all the electrical jobs, like meter reading, were all handled by white men. The job required driving a truck into a white neighborhood, walking on homeowners' property, and going around to the back of the house to read the meter. During those times, a Black person could not walk on a white person's property, so only white men were given that job.

For the same reason, the milk men and mail carriers were all white. Similarly, a "Colored" man—as Black people were called during the 1950s and 1960s—could not be a police officer with the authority to carry a gun, enforce the law and shoot people.

The milk man and mail carriers were friendly and talked with me and my parents. While white people were expected to adhere to the segregation laws, many white people appeared tired of discrimination. One white man frequently drove slowly through our neighborhood in his red convertible Cadillac, stopping to chat with any adult. Sometimes when my mom was sitting outside, making a quilt, he would stop and strike up a conversation.

When I went grocery shopping with my parents, many stores prohibited Colored people from entering. However, as I recall, two white brothers created two grocery stores where any person could shop. They were the Cotten family. I remember that one brother was named Fred and the other Jimmy. Over in Waskom, Texas, the only grocery store was operated by the Hall family. It, too, was open to any person.

When segregation ended with the 1964 Civil Rights Act, Colored people were reluctant to patronize Kroger. Their prices for goods were higher and most importantly, across the street was Cotten's store. It had a well-established, good history with Colored people. Kroger closed its store at this location.

As I recall, Colored people could only shop for clothes, shoes and accessories in downtown Shreveport stores on Saturday morning. The stores were on Texas Avenue, the main street which ended at a big Baptist church made of red brick with white trim.

When the church bell rang at noon on Saturdays, that was the warning for Colored people to be out of the stores and in their vehicles parked on each side of Texas Avenue, ready to leave downtown. Then the store clerks prepared for the white customers.

When the state fair came to town every October, white people attended on specified days, and Colored people went to the fair on days allocated for us. No white people came on the Colored people's day. As we went through the park, we were served without any racial problems. And we understood that the best way to avoid conflicts was to "stay in our place."

One of my favorite places to visit in Shreveport—to this day—is the Southern Maid Donuts. Made hot to order, the donuts melt in your mouth and are unbelievably delicious. Well, back when I was a child, the store had a parakeet. As a Colored person entered the shop, the bird announced, "N***** in the store!"

We ignored it and found it comical. Plus, the quality of the donuts far overrode the bird's racial slur.

Today, my wife Sheila and I still go to Southern Maid Donuts to enjoy these incredibly delicious treats. And oh, by the way, the parakeet is long gone.

On a more serious note, I do not recall there being a Colored dentist in Shreveport; the first time I went to the dentist was when I was 22 years old and living in Michigan. Dr. Pogoncheff was my first dentist and is still the dentist for my wife and me to this day!

When I was growing up, I only saw white medical people. When we went to the doctor, we had to enter through the entrance marked "Colored," not the door that said, "Whites Only." Any person of color was required to go to the Colored waiting room.

It was the same experience at the bus station, which had a big waiting area for white folks that included a restaurant and pinball machines. In the back of the bus station was the "Colored" waiting room, where folks were met with fumes from fuel, smoke and diesel buses blowing over them. This waiting room that had one or two seats was the size of a closet and the drinking fountain was located outdoors.

Despite these circumstances, we didn't have many racial problems because we did not have much contact with white people.

However, we heard about bad things happening to Colored people.

The news reported that some white men had attacked a Colored man, captured him, tied his hands behind his back with a chain, tied his feet together and dropped him in the lake. We also heard about one of our coaches who whistled at a white woman, who reported it to the police. He was chased, captured, beaten and jailed.

When we heard about things like this, we were quiet and couldn't do anything about it.

We did not use racial name calling in our family. However, I had heard other Colored people refer to white people as "crackers." When I moved to Michigan as an adult, while mingling with white people, I heard them use the term "white trash." This tickled me that a white person would call another white person such a slang term. My response, however, was that I didn't want to know any more name-calling and said, "Please don't tell me any other slang names."

My brother Albany remembers a poignant moment involving Dad delivering a package to the home of the wealthiest white man in Waskom. The custom back in the fifties in the South was for Colored people to go to the back door of any white person's house.

"I am not going to the back door of this man's house," Dad announced to 10-year-old Albany, who sat in the passenger seat, as they drove to the house. "If he wants his package, he will come to the front door!"

Were they scared? Oh, yes!

Oh, boy, Albany thought.

Dad pulled up in the circular driveway, walked to the front door with the package in hand and rang the doorbell.

Albany stayed in the vehicle and watched fearfully. Neither Dad nor Albany knew what was going to happen, yet they readied themselves for confrontation either immediately or later. This was back in the day of Jim Crow laws, written and unwritten, that could get a Colored man killed for the slightest offense to a white person.

Albany's heart was pounding and Dad's probably was as well. Dad treated others with respect and recognized their importance. He wanted others to do the same for him.

"My father grew up in a time where Colored people had restricted rights," said my oldest brother Albany, 79, an author who lives in Chicago, during an interview for this book. "Looking at life through my father's eyes demanded courage, rational thought, and the ability to say, 'Yes, sir,' and 'Yes, ma'am,' even when he didn't mean it."

Albany continued, "A better life for Dad was his belief in God, hard work, family and hope for a better tomorrow. Even though viewed by some white Americans as worthless, shiftless, lazy and less than three-fifths of a man, those concepts were far from his ideals of self and the broader community of Black people."

With that in mind, Dad stood courageously on this white man's front porch, defying the laws of the land. After a few minutes, the white man opened the door, took the package and said to Dad, **"Thank you, sir."**

What a relief for Dad and Albany!

I am proud of Albany and grateful that he shared this memory.

Here's the ironic twist to this story. While Albany and Dad never went inside that white man's house, I spent time inside the home for the first five or so years of my life, and played with this white man's daughters. How did this happen? This was the same home where my cousin Ragland worked as a maid and took me to work with her on Saturdays.

The South and its racial structure presented challenges to Colored people and more to Colored men to achieve much and live above poverty. Yet, Dad and others rose above the low standards for Colored men. Dad showed that when you keep yourself focused on some good reasons to work and to possess things, much could be accomplished, though in small amounts. **Yes, there were inequalities, there were lots of stereotypes for Colored people and the way we should live, and injustices, yet, my parents and others kept going forward.**

My dad and mom never hung their heads low with an attitude that *the sky is falling on me*. What I concluded was that their strength came from within themselves, making them believe that they could succeed in difficult circumstances. Their fortitude did not come from external sources such as titles, rank or associations.

TV BRINGS JOY

Dad's income enabled him to purchase a TV that provided endless entertainment in our home. We were the first in our family to have a TV, and my cousin Oscar fondly remembers coming to our house with his siblings to enjoy the shows and sports matches with us.

"Uncle D was the first one who got a TV back in 1952," Oscar recalled. "TV was the best thing in the world. We'd sneak down there on the weekends and watch TV. I loved *The Honeymooners* with Jackie Gleason. 'Don't yawl stay too long,' Momma said. Kids would watch TV all night if you let them."

Our first TV was on a stand with wheels. Then we got a 27-inch screen. In time, we acquired a bigger, one-piece console. All were black and white.

The TV was in the den/family room, and excited cheers filled our home as we watched sports. Then we laughed a lot while watching comic shows such as *I Love Lucy*, *The Andy Griffith Show*, *McHale's Navy*, and so on. We felt scared watching *The Twilight Zone* and *Alfred Hitchcock Presents*.

On Saturday mornings, I watched cartoons featuring Bugs Bunny, Casper the Ghost and the Road Runner.

Saturday afternoons brought Dad into the den to watch professional baseball games. After completing his chores around the house, he was ready to relax in his chair. Wearing a baseball cap, he'd sit in his chair with an unlit cigar in his mouth and watch his favorite sport. On the best days, he got to watch his favorite player, Willie Mays, Jr., the Alabama native and center fielder who played Major League Baseball for the New York Mets, the San Francisco Giants and the New York Giants.

Dad loved the game of professional baseball. He enjoyed watching it both on TV and in person when an exhibition professional game was played in Shreveport. Dad often spoke about being a pitcher and how he felt he had some talent.

Dad had this dream while living at a time when many young, southern Colored men did not dream big and when many desires for achievement went unfulfilled. Any hopes and dreams of being a professional baseball player would not materialize for reasons outside of Dad's control. During his boyhood, young Colored boys could dream and speak of their dreams only to others who could not direct or help them move closer to the dream becoming a reality.

We mostly watched the St. Louis Cardinals, as the Atlanta Braves were not yet publicized much. Sometimes we watched west coast teams—the Los Angeles Dodgers and the San Francisco Giants.

"That's a strike!" Dad would exclaim. He'd also cheer when somebody made a great play.

Meanwhile, I watched on the couch while Mom was in the kitchen. It was the two of us, as far back as I can remember, enjoying those games together. During commercials, we'd run into the kitchen and get bologna sandwiches, or just bologna or hot dogs or wieners that we bought ready-to-eat from a store in Texas. Baseball games were a fun time for son and Dad.

As a family, we watched western movies on Saturday

night, including *Gunsmoke, Palladin, Rawhide, Wells Fargo* and *Wagon Train.* I still watch those today.

Sometimes our Saturday night viewing included a boxing match featuring Floyd Patterson, George Foreman, Cassius Clay, Joe Frazier or Sonny Liston.

Our parents sat in chairs and us kids squeezed onto the couch. We also brought in chairs from the dining room and kitchen so everyone could squeeze into the family room. There was a lot of noise and excitement. Most of the time, only Patricia, Raymond and I were there, because Albany and Sylvia had moved out and Albert wasn't home much. He had a girlfriend.

Even though I was excited to watch TV, I was quiet. I just liked to watch and listen.

Later in life, the color TV became available, and my sister Pat and her husband purchased one for Dad and Mom.

HIGHER EDUCATION IS KEY TO SUCCESS

Everyone—our families, people at church and in the neighborhood, and our teachers—encouraged us to, "Get your education so you can make something of yourself."

Our community had many teachers, a carpenter, a masonry contractor, and a few men who worked on the passenger train. Many of them had attended Historically Black Colleges and Universities (HBCUs) such as Texas Southern University, Wiley College and Bishop College.

During my upbringing, many Black people of Dad and Mom's age were not high school graduates. Their formal educations varied widely. Some completed elementary school; some went several grade levels in high school. As a kid, and still today, I am amazed at the accomplishments of so many Black people living in the South with its many restrictions.

My older siblings, who graduated from Walnut Hill High School, where Dad was president of the Band Parent Club, also set an example to attend college. Albany was the first son to attend college. Albert did for two years, then joined the U.S. Navy. Two of my brothers received music scholarships to Mississippi Valley State University.

My sister Pat went there without a scholarship for a year, then moved to Lansing, Michigan. Sylvia attended Grambling State University for one semester, then returned to Shreveport for beauty college.

My first time going to a college graduation was for one of my first cousins; I believe it was Uncle Buddy and Aunt Viola's oldest child. She was 16 years old when I was born, so I was still young at her graduation. We went to Grambling College for her graduation; I remember being in awe of the pretty campus with its many buildings. As I grew older, I remembered that moment with great gratitude as I learned how important Grambling was to the Black students wanting to receive a college degree.

At that time, the HBCUs were recruiting many of the more talented athletes and this helped the schools receive general and athletic recognition. Dad and Mom tried to support as many of their nieces and nephews as possible. My Uncle Buddy and Aunt Viola did not have much money to live on daily. Somehow, they managed to help several of their nine children attend and graduate from college. My immediate family and extended family did not talk much about the difficult things to do, they just did it.

Dad and his brothers all served in the military. With this history known to Dad's nephews, many of them also served in the military. They all returned home safe and well. Many times, an example speaks volumes. This is what I believed Dad's and his brothers' examples did for those nephews and two of my brothers.

ENJOYING SCHOOL WHILE FREE FROM SHADOWS

My sister Sylvia, as the oldest child, was 10 years older than me. The age differences between us children contributed to some good and bad things during our upbringing. My older siblings had to deal with shadows, whereas I did not.

Living in someone's shadow can be a hindrance or set standards for you. You're always trying to prove yourself. I didn't have that. It allowed me that freeness to be me and to grow. And I didn't have the teachers saying, "Oh, you're such-and-such's brother." Plus, I could make my own friends.

Four of my siblings attended a school for grades one through 12. I, along with my third-oldest brother Albert, attended Greenmoor Elementary School for grades one through six. When I started elementary school, my brother Albert was in the fifth grade. He did not leave a shadow for me.

Greenmoor Elementary (now under a new name) was set in a rural area. It was about 15-plus miles from our home. I rode the yellow school bus each school day. I attended the school without siblings leading the way. This was a very enjoyable time period. I was free to grow and develop without being in someone else's shadow.

After Greenmoor Elementary, I completed grades seven through 12 at Walnut Hill High School. Junior high and high school were part of the makeup of Walnut Hill High School. It, like Greenmoor, was set in a rural area. Very clean and well-kept. My graduating class was somewhere close to 100 students, give or take a few. While I was in the 7th grade, my sister, Patricia, and brother, Albert, were still students at the school, yet several grades above me. Once again, I rode the yellow school bus each school day.

Our Aunt Daisy was a teacher at the school and Patricia would ride to and from school with her. In the afternoon, Aunt Daisy would visit briefly with Mom before she drove home. Perhaps that was stress relief for Aunt Daisy. I do not recall how Albert got to and from school. This again provided me with freeness to be myself and grow and develop without being in someone else's shadow.

I enjoyed my formative schooling. It gave me my strong, enduring foundation that I stand on and operate from today.

My older brother, as the second child, was in the shadows of others for a long time. He and my dad shared the same first name (Albany). Dad did not have a middle name. My brother Albany has a middle name. Based upon the shared first name, people called my brother "Junior." This would last until "Junior" was roughly 40 years old. He was in Dad's shadow. He reached the point where he would ask people to call him by his first name, Albany.

Lesson learned by me! I saw both good and bad about Shadows. I decided and applied in my life that my wife and children would not have shadows governing their lives. To me, when a shadow is too small, it can limit growth, experiences, and opportunities. When a shadow is too large, it can create unreachable feats and goals.

I learned some personal character lessons while in school.

A significant event, perhaps the death of Dr. Martin Luther King, Jr., prompted some of us students to decide to walk out of class and stand in protest. I walked out with my classmates. Then I suddenly perceived the kids walking out around me as "losers." They were not smart or quality kids. So, I turned around and went back in class, because I didn't want to be associated with those kids.

Another time, I witnessed a fellow student's verbal attack on our chemistry teacher, who was really skinny and did not appear able to defend himself physically. A kid who was not in our class decided to come in and interrupt our class. The teacher asked him to leave. The student launched a verbal attack, refusing to leave. The teacher went to the principal's office to get this student to leave.

Then the teacher filed a charge against the student.

They asked for eyewitnesses from the 12 students in our class. Nobody said anything and acted like they hadn't seen anything. I saw the whole thing.

"I'll be your eyewitness," I said.

The case went to a court hearing before a judge. Before it started, I went to the restroom. The student was there. I told him the truth—that he made a big mistake. I didn't have any fear of him, even though he was bigger than me. I thought, *I could take him myself.*

When the judge asked me to testify, I told him exactly what I had seen. The judge put the guy in jail over the weekend for harassing the teacher.

Back at school, I had some classes with the guy's twin brother. (He also had another brother who was hot-headed and some sisters who had reputations for being tough.)

"Oh, when he gets out," kids taunted me, "he's gonna get you!"

The guy lived a short walk across the highway and I thought, *All I had to do was go to his house and take care of him.*

When he got out of jail and came back to school, he was like a lamb. Jail took care of him. We never had any fights.

I was hoping that his jail time served as an example for his brothers to stay out of trouble. And I was glad that

I had the courage to stand up for what was right.

CHORES & OBSERVATIONS TEACH IMPORTANT LESSONS

We washed clothes on Saturday mornings. Before we purchased a washing machine, we washed and rinsed clothes by hand, then hung all the items outdoors on the clothes lines. Neither of my sisters liked this manual labor, and I was too young to help. When my time came, we had purchased a washing machine that was part mechanical and manual. It made the laundry chore easier. Hanging the laundry was not a problem for me.

In fact, I never minded doing any chores, because they taught me important lessons about how a strong work ethic leads to a positive outcome, and that I had the power to make decisions to influence my life's circumstances. For example, I liked having a clean kitchen and clean silverware, so when I learned to wash dishes, Mom didn't have to say anything to me. I can't say the same for all my siblings.

"Sylvia, it's your turn to do the dishes," Mom would say.

But my sisters didn't like washing dishes by hand, so Mom would have to fuss: "Sylvia, you go on and do these dishes!"

Mom showed me how to clean the house, cook and iron clothes. To this day, I like to dust and keep things tidy. My brother Albany is the cleanest one of the family; he's particular about everything and wants it very clean.

Mom made sure that us siblings, as well as Dad, knew how to care for ourselves.

Dad didn't repair cars or lawn mowers, so us boys didn't pick up any of that type of stuff.

However, my older brothers learned how to plow with the mule. I never plowed. When I grew in size and gained strength, we were no longer using a mule.

I learned to drive by observing how my father drove a manual shift vehicle with the gear on the steering wheel, and how to use the clutch and accelerator by coordinating the right foot with the left foot on the clutch. Some people, when learning to drive a manual shift vehicle, stall it out, but I didn't, because I had watched Dad do it hundreds of times.

One afternoon after school, when I was 15, Mom let me drive the car by myself and I succeeded by imitating exactly what I had seen Dad do. I reached a speed of 70 mph on that two-lane highway, which had a lower speed limit. Youthful thinking!

NOT FOLLOWING RAYMOND'S EXAMPLE

Raymond did not respond well to advice from Dad and Mom. He was more inclined to listen to his peers.

"Don't run with the wrong crowd," Dad warned over and over.

"Don't get with the wrong crowd," Mom repeated, referring to classmates who cut class and got such bad grades that they failed a grade.

All of us listened except Raymond, who had a repu-tation for being hard-headed. He thought it was cool to hang with the kids at school who shared cigarettes in the boys' bathroom. We knew this because Aunt Daisy was a teacher at the school.

"Stay away from fast girls," Mom warned Raymond, who ended up pursuing and later marrying a woman whom he didn't respect.

Raymond also ignored Dad's frequent warning: "If you get put in jail, I won't bail you out."

After Raymond graduated from high school, he wanted to go straight to work and start earning money. When he got paid on payday, he would stay out all night and come home a day or so later—dead broke! He was 18 or 19 years old. That would hurt my mom and dad tre-mendously. Mom would fuss at him and try to get him to see that, "You need money to buy gas to put in your car to go to work," and, "You need to save some money."

She also told him, "If you would just come home and give me a piece of your check, I will save it for you."

That could not get through his head. Each payday, he would do the same thing, showing up dead broke. I would sit there and listen as my mom fussed. I learned from that, thinking, *I don't want to follow in Raymond's footsteps.*

One day after his payday, Raymond called.

"I'm in jail," Raymond said.

Guess where he was in jail! Not in Shreveport where we lived, but almost 400 miles away in Oklahoma! He asked

Dad to come bail him out. This was Dad's big moment to let Raymond learn a hard but valuable lesson.

Dad had a decision to make: let Raymond stay in jail, be absent from work, possibly lose his job and suffer other consequences. Dad fussed around the house as he talked the matter over with Mom. I knew he would let Raymond stay in jail, just as he warned him many times.

Dad decided to bail Raymond out of jail. Was that the best decision? Did Dad help Raymond to learn a hard but valuable lesson? Mom supported Dad's choice. Raymond came home embarrassed and humbled and as a result, he made some improvements to his life.

As a kid, I attentively listened to my parents. Their directions and advice to me and my siblings made sense. As I grew up with their insights, it was easier to select between good and bad. Even today, I'm still selecting the good outcome.

Chapter 2 — Contentment

⁂

I knew my dad for 63 years. Eighteen of those years were spent growing into manhood around him and Mom. It was during those years that Dad introduced me to making "rooted" decisions. That is to say, decisions that are well-established and have shown to produce good results.

Contentment to Dad meant awakening to peaceful conditions, with good food to eat and useful/beneficial things to do throughout the day. When it was time for him to relax, he enjoyed sitting on the carport with his legs crossed and his cigar in his mouth. Other times, he enjoyed watching a baseball game with his cigar in his mouth, which was unlit most of the time. He loved wearing some type of baseball-style cap.

As mentioned before, Dad loved the game of professional baseball. He enjoyed watching it both on TV and in person when a professional exhibition game was played in Shreveport. Dad often spoke about being a pitcher when he was young, and how he felt he had some talent. This was him sharing one of his dreams. Dad lived at a time when many young southern Colored men did not dream big and when many desires for achievement would go unfulfilled. Any hopes and dreams of his being a professional baseball player would not materialize for reasons outside of his control. During his boyhood, young Colored boys could dream and speak of their dreams only to others who could not direct or help them move closer to the dream becoming a reality.

Something better came for him. He was able to see many other Black men reach some of their dreams. His favorite professional baseball player was none other than, you guessed it, Willie Mays.

Dad never met any of the professional baseball players. He never traveled to see the famous stadiums. He never received a game ball. Yet, he was contented with his reach in life. He spent his life enjoying professional baseball primarily through the television.

Nowadays, people can realize their dreams. Any lack of achievement or growth has to be more squarely placed on each person's efforts.

As a husband, Dad was challenged with providing for a wife and children and as the years passed, Mom would succumb to the effects of diabetes and other ailments. Their knowledge and understanding of those ailments were minimal at best. Dad and Mom followed her doctor's treatment. This brought Dad contentment to know that he did his best in caring for Mom. They loved fishing and working in the garden together. Those activities were performed early in the morning and late in the evening. The yields of their efforts not only fed us, but also allowed them to be generous and share with others.

His parenting style was showing, doing by example. He used very few words to explain or teach a point. Dad was not big on dispensing wisdom or sitting down having a one-on-one conversation about life with his children. However, one by one, each of us six children received the parenting that was needed to be mature, respectful, and useful people in society. This brought contentment to both Dad and Mom.

Dad, at times, did share his wisdom with other family members.

"He was very influential on me," said Cousin Charles. "We had things in common because he was an ex-military man and I was in the military. When I was just starting out, he advised me to buy some land next to him. He said, 'I want you to buy this land, boy. I want to know who I'm living next to. Give them a down payment.' I took his advice and purchased this land."

Charles, who was married and stationed in the U.S. Air Force in Mississippi and then sent to Vietnam, built a house on the property beside my parents' home in 1971.

"I had no worries about my wife, Laverne, and the house because Uncle D was there," Charles said. Likewise, when the sink sprung a leak while Charles was away, he said Uncle D came over and fixed it for Laverne. Uncle D was a good family man. When Charles was home, he said Uncle D would step out to the hurricane fence between the houses.

"Uncle D would call, 'Hey boy, come on over here.' And we talked over the fence about politics. He was crazy about baseball and loved the Atlanta Braves and the San Francisco Giants. He talked about his favorite player, Willie Mays."

Charles remembered one of Dad's sayings. "When I asked him, 'Uncle D, how are you doing?' He had a saying: 'Everything is normal!' I figured out that meant, 'Everything is okay.'"

Charles said Dad also provided career guidance by saying, "'Boy, you need to stay in the service. You're a young man. Stay 20 years, then by the time you're 40 years old, you can start another occupation.' He gave me advice about life: 'Boy, you still got a life ahead of you.'"

Dad's advice to Charles spanned friendships and marriage.

"He always told me, 'Boy, you gotta stay away from bad folks.' He would encourage me when I had difficulties with marriage by saying, 'Boy, you gotta do this push and pull.' He gave good, valuable information about how to get along with folks." Charles was a special nephew of Dad, and Uncle Buddy's first son.

After Charles retired in 1980, he said, "I used to help Uncle D cut the grass around the church and in the graveyard. He was on the graveyard committee. He did a lot of work and he was a hard-working man."

As the years passed and Dad aged, Charles cut Dad's yard and looked after him. "I told Uncle D, 'Every time you want to get your medicine, I'll get it. You don't have to drive anywhere. I'm going to be there for you, Uncle D. I won't leave. I'm going to take care of you.'"

As I mentioned earlier, Dad went to work with peace, day after day. His job or work never defined who he was or measured his worth as a person. To this day, I have never known of any work title that Dad held. He never spoke of any work title of any person at his place of employment.

He achieved contentment without a title. That was his example.

Doing his best and sharing with others brought Dad years of contentment.

Chapter 3 — Work

D̲ad's last employment upon retirement was with Ralston Purina Company in Shreveport, Louisiana. He was hired in March of 1954 and retired in February of 1982.

Dad never talked to me about his place of employment, his work, or any of his work associates. In today's time, we can be filled with joy and excitement over a promotion, a transfer, a pay raise and many other uplifting work opportunities. This would not be my dad's experience.

I merely saw him get up early, clean up, eat breakfast, and go off to work. He would return home later in the afternoon/evening. Dad worked some Saturdays.

Dad's workplace was segregated, as Colored men were relegated to the most difficult and dangerous jobs. When Dad worked at Ralston Purina in the feed division, they put Colored men in one area—on the dock alongside a railroad spur.

The Colored men manually loaded the railcar with animal food. They had no forklift. They had to use their backs and muscles to load heavy bags of feed. They also manually loaded semi-tractor trailer trucks. My Uncle Buddy worked there awhile. He didn't have the strength of my dad and died in his eighties.

At the job, the supervisor was always white. My dad stayed out of racial problems.

Once a year, his employer sponsored a family Saturday barbecue somewhere close to Cross Lake. We enjoyed this outing very much. Sometimes Dad would assist with the barbecuing. It was fun to play the games, listen to conversations, and visit with different people.

Dad never complained about his work, employer, or any of his work associates. This proved to be very useful to me. When I entered the work force, my initial goal was to look for positive things at work and in each person. That way, I would also work without much complaining.

Dad always left early for work, so as not to be late. I followed this same pattern. Dad came home tired, yet ready to help with lawn mowing and working in the family garden.

As far as I can remember, Dad did not take any sick days from work. He sometimes caught a cold, yet it did not stop him from going to work. This was not true of me. I missed some work because of sickness.

Dad worked at Ralston Purina for 27 years and 11 months—almost 28 years. His work example led to several of his children having long work careers with one employer. We are thankful for his example and lead.

Upon Dad's retirement, although he did not know it, he would have only three more years of marriage with Mom, as she would die in 1985. Dad spent those three years enjoying a simple and relaxed life with Mom. They enjoyed visiting with local family members and friends of all ages, as well as going to church.

During his nearly 28 years at Ralston Purina, Dad received a weekly paycheck. After that, he enjoyed nearly a 34-year retirement, receiving a monthly pension check. Work for almost 28 years and get paid for 34 more, adding up to (28 + 34) nearly 62 years. Not bad!

Overall, Dad set the bar high for his family to follow (years of work, attendance at work, years of retirement). His employment included working during a time of segregation. At the company-sponsored Saturday barbecue, only Colored people attended. By the time Dad retired, segregation had ended per law.

Dad's legacy to us was this: *When you first begin your work history, it will be different from your ending. You can handle each change, adjustment, and challenge that comes along.*

Dad retired with a pension, Social Security, and some healthcare benefits. Work was fulfilling to him. He retired fulfilled and happy.

Chapter 4 — Money

❧

Dad used his earned income to support himself and his family. When he purchased a vehicle, he would drive it for many years—sometimes as many as 20 or more years. He oftentimes used self-taught mechanics to service and repair his vehicles. Dad drove GM vehicles mostly; once he owned a Chrysler.

Dad drove his green truck and brown Oldsmobile for more than 15 years. This rubbed off on my brother Albany and me. Back in 2020, we had been driving our respective vehicles for more than 17 years. Have we gotten our money's worth? We are grateful for Dad's example of maintaining his vehicles and of getting his money's worth. By the way, I had to replace my 19-year-old Honda with a new 2020 Buick in late 2020.

Dad's earned income was low, yet he continuously made his money go a long way and to handle many responsibilities (paying bills, giving to church causes, caring for self and family, and helping other people in need). He worked long hours to earn his wages. He would patiently wait until he could save the money to buy most of the things needed. He did learn to use the system of Lay-Away.

Even though he was a low-income earner, we always had what we needed. We lived thriftily and cared for the material things we had, and they remained useable and in good repair for long periods of time.

My mom had inherited property in Texas from her mother. That property had oil and gas on it. My mom and grandmother had signed mineral rights contracts. This enabled my mom to receive royalty payments through-out the year. That income, along with my dad's income, helped us to buy the things we needed.

Dad enjoyed having some money in his pockets. He never complained about money or his lot in life. Impressing others with money or with its purchasing power was of no importance to him. Dad almost never talked about money. He did not give me advice about saving or earning money. He led by example. In his later years of life, we came to learn of him having a small amount of money saved in the bank.

His money allowed him to be self-sufficient, meeting his needs and those of his family along with some wants. Money did not define Dad or establish his value or worth.

Dad never gained much experience from making financial investments. His money management came from earning, saving, and some spending. His basic money management skills along with trustworthiness resulted in his being given the responsibility to collect and deposit the church's monies into its bank account.

With some of his money, Dad would buy vegetable seeds and then plant a large garden. (When you are a child, any garden plot can look large, but this one was!) The garden would produce enough food for us to eat immediately, freeze to last through the winter, and share with others.

Dad reached the point where he did not need to add additional income. His monthly retirement income was enough to allow him and his wife to live happily and not worry about outliving his income.

When I moved out of my parents' house, Dad gave me roughly $92 as a grubstake. My sister Pat and her husband asked me if I wanted to move in with them in Lansing, Michigan. Wow, how that has proven to be an unending blessing.

That $92 was stretched so far and for so long, that I never ran out of money. I was very motivated to find a job and carry my own weight. This, I did, and am still doing—Dad and Mom's example at work.

Dad never discussed with me the subjects of money, how much to earn, how much to save, how much to give, or how much to spend. He did not discuss or encourage investing money or the value of compound interest. I believe he understood very little about money matters other than working to earn money, paying bills, and saving only a small amount of money in the bank. Yet, Dad was never broke, nor did he ask others for their money.

Money was not King over Dad. He used money to meet the needs of his family. We always had what we needed. Most importantly, Dad was happy with the way he managed money. He never complained about money.

As Dad aged, and especially around 96, he could no longer manage his affairs well. Yet he still had some money in his savings account and he continued to receive his pension and social security income. Dad never ran out of money.

My brother, Albert, and my dad in the backyard barbecuing with four grills.

Family in the backyard, enjoying each other's company.

Dad, his nephew, Charles, and his son-in-law, Leon, (right to left) in the side yard, enjoying beverages and a snack.

My sister, Sylvia, and her daughter, DeShawn, on graduation day.

In California visiting Dad's brother, Nathaniel, shown with Vernon and great niece, Jerran. Left to right: Nathaniel, Jerran and me (Vernon).

At brother Albany's wedding. Left to right: Dad's second-oldest brother, Ernest Sr.; his wife, Viola; Dad's oldest sister, Lola; my oldest sibling, Sylvia; and (standing) Albany and his wife, Madelyn.

Dad at his workplace, Ralston Purina (top left next to train).

Dad and Mom at my wedding in 1975 when Dad was 55 years old.

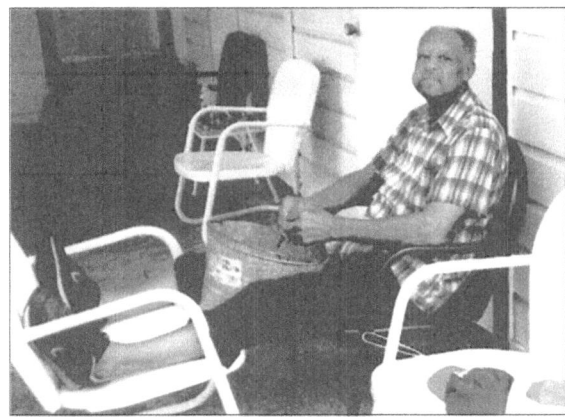

Dad on carport shelling peas and chewing tobacco.

Chapter 5 — Trees

After Dad and Mom purchased property in Greenwood Acres Subdivision and built our house, they planted two pecan trees, a peach tree, two plum trees, and a pear tree in the backyard.

As a young child, I saw those trees grow and produce nuts and fruits respectively, ranging from small to large amounts. The plum trees were the first in the spring to produce fruit. Next came the peaches, then the pears, and finally the pecans in the fall. We harvested the fresh produce from spring into the fall.

Once the pecans came, we would eat them often, give many away, and store some to eat throughout the winter. We would eat until we were tired of them. I cracked them open the way my dad did it, by placing two pecans in one hand, and squeezing them together until they cracked. I preferred this method over the more cumbersome nutcracker.

If I wanted a snack after school, I could gather pecans from the yard, build a pile, crack them open, and stick them in my mouth. Our garden also provided plenty of snacks throughout the warmer months. So, you'd go from eating plums to strawberries, then wait awhile and eat peaches, and in the fall, pecans.

We also grew peanuts, which were another favorite after school snack. Peanuts grow on a plant. The soil stays moist while the plant is in the dirt. At harvest time for peanuts, you pull the plant up, turn it over, put the plant on its back, expose the nuts to the sun, and allow them to dry out. You let them sit for a day or so, then shake all the dust off the plant and nuts. You could eat them raw or put them on a cookie sheet and roast in the oven a few minutes to have roasted peanuts.

We never went hungry! Both Mom and Dad had an agricultural background as kids, so they could apply it as parents.

None of the trees required much care. I do not recall specifically fertilizing any of the trees. The care we provided included regular lawn care and some pruning of limbs and raking of leaves.

Those trees stayed healthy and produced into my adulthood. Eventually the plum trees were cut down, and so was the peach tree. The pecan trees kept on producing, even after my parents became empty nesters. Mom would collect a grocery bag full of pecans and ship them to me and some of my siblings.

Those trees provided us with many life lessons. The trees grew slowly each year and they produced according to their size and strength. This is the life lesson Dad and Mom taught us. We were better off to pursue growth in quality of life slowly instead of chasing after the big pay-out. This lesson helped us to better receive, understand and handle the growth and success.

By having trees that required low care, this lesson helped us to pursue opportunities that would not consume the majority of our time. We could have time to devote to a variety of matters, such as family needs, religious needs, work and so on.

The pecan trees are still on the property. This shows that there are many things in life that we want to last for a long time, or even to last for decades after we are deceased. We are encouraged to leave a good legacy. Do things that are bigger than us.

The trees grew to provide shade for us to enjoy sitting under while having many conversations with others. They also provided a clean-up opportunity in the fall for raking the leaves. I enjoyed this. My sister Patricia did not. It was an unwelcome chore to her.

Birds often flew into and out of those trees. Those trees were and are the gift that keeps giving. As the trees grew taller, they grew more branches. This lesson showed us that as we grew older, bigger and stronger, we needed to take on greater responsibilities. We also had to care for those responsibilities, just as the trees cared for the branches. Did Dad or Mom have all of these lessons in mind when they planted those trees? Whether they did or not, this turned out to be a very practical and thrifty means of living off the land.

Our homeland produced food of some type for us to eat continually throughout the year. This lesson showed us it is not always how large something must be, but more importantly, it is how wisely you use something that will determine its value and outcome.

These life lessons can be used by any person and are always current with each generation.

Chapter 6 — Quietly Proud

❦

Neither Dad nor Mom boasted or bragged about any of their accomplishments or the accomplishments of any of their children or other relatives.

When my older brother Albany, the firstborn son of the family, was accepted to college at Mississippi Valley State, and later was preparing for his graduation, our parents were quietly proud. They humbly told relatives about Albany's achievement, and discreetly planned a trip to Mississippi to attend his college graduation.

I had never been to Mississippi. I was excited to make the trip, yet I was scared because of the bad racial-related things. I had heard about many hurtful things happening to Black people. We made the trip without problem.

On the way to the college, and during our return trip home, neither Dad nor Mom spoke of their joy or happiness of Albany's achievement. However, I am sure that, inside, they were each leaping for joy.

Both Dad and Mom were very proud of my brother Albert being in the Navy. He sent home a picture of himself in a leather military jacket, and Mom quietly made the picture available for others to see when they visited us and asked how Albert was doing.

My older sister Sylvia moved from Louisiana to Michigan, then got engaged, married, and became the first to become a parent and give my parents a grandchild. All of these high points brought such joy to the family. Dad and Mom quietly told others of these high points.

This discreet proudness manifested itself throughout my upbringing. I learned not to boast or brag about myself or any of my family members. Rather, I quietly appreciated each accomplishment.

Those accomplishments included attending college and embarking on a long and successful career, both of which were influenced by my siblings' accomplishments and geographic locations.

Five of us children attended college. Two of us became college graduates. All of us contributed to society as employed people helping to provide needed services. Five of us raised children and many of them are college graduates.

Two of my sisters created a path that ultimately took me to Lansing, Michigan. After my sister Pat went to Mississippi Valley State without a scholarship for a year, she moved to Lansing, which is the state capital of Michigan. Sylvia attended Grambling State University for one semester, then returned to Shreveport for beauty college, where the owner trained ladies how to become beauticians. In Lansing, my mom's first cousin was a beautician and owned a shop. One summer, while vacationing in Shreveport, she invited Sylvia to move to Michigan, which she did. Then Sylvia was employed in our cousin's beauty shop in Lansing. This expanded Sylvia's horizon and opened the door for Pat to go to Lansing, and that opened the door for me to move there as well.

But first, after I graduated from high school at age 17, I attended Louisiana Tech University for one year. Then, that summer, I moved to Michigan and was hired by Meijer, a retail store. Shortly afterward, I started working for the State of Michigan's Department of Treasury. After saving some money, I enrolled in college at Lansing Community College (LCC). Upon completion of my studies at LCC, I then applied for admission to Wayne State University (WSU) and Michigan State University (MSU). I heard first from WSU and went there for one semester. While at WSU, I received acceptance to attend MSU, where I earned my Bachelor of Arts degree in Communications.

Because I was working for the state, I calculated the cost of tuition for my classes each semester, then saved the money from my job to pay for it. As a result, I did not owe any money when I graduated.

Then, while researching what I should do with my degree in MSU's Student Placement Building, I learned that I could use my communications degree in the insurance industry. I really wanted to go to Aetna in Hartford, Connecticut. It was a big company that had a history of working with, developing, and promoting Black people. I also liked what I read about Auto-Owners Insurance Company in Lansing. So, dressed like a college student, I went to Auto-Owners one afternoon, stepped into the personnel department, and asked about career ladder opportunities.

"We don't have any information like that," a manager told me, adding, "I want you to go home and change clothes and come back."

So, I did. He interviewed me. He set up three additional interviews with three more people on another day. I interviewed with them. Then, I received a job offer in the mail. I accepted the job and was hired on October 23, 1978.

Still, I wondered, *Is this the way God wants me to go?* At the time, Auto-Owners Insurance Company employed few Black people. In time, we added more employees (associates) from diverse backgrounds.

I stayed and worked through a lot of things, and after 36 years with the company, retired on November 1, 2014.

As for Aetna, the company looked so good from the outside, but shortly after starting my insurance career, the Property Casualty part of Aetna was gone. If I had taken a job there, I would have lost a job. I was happy that I had not gone there.

Throughout my career, I emulated my father's quiet proudness.

Quiet proudness means recognizing the work, efforts, achievements, joys, excitements of a person and then telling them how they are appreciated.

Dad did not tell us with words how we were appreciated; he showed it with his actions. He would pat you on the back or shoulder.

Chapter 7 — Silent Leader

$\mathcal{A}$s Dad lived 98 years, 11 months, and 19 days, he lived through many historical events. He was one year old around the beginning of the Spanish Influenza in 1918. He went on to live through such major events as:

· The Great Depression;
· World War I;
· World War II;
· The Korean War;
· The Vietnam War;
· The invention of television;
· Civil unrest around the U.S., such as riots in Detroit and Los Angeles;
· Civil rights marches;
· The killing of Reverend Dr. Martin Luther King, Jr.;

· The killing of President John F. Kennedy; and
· The killing of Presidential Candidate Robert F. Kennedy.

Each of those events changed Dad's disposition. As Dad aged, he saw a lot, heard a lot, and experienced many troubling emotions as difficult events occurred in the World. Dad remained silent during the events that occurred during my life. He was raised in racial segregation in Louisiana, during which Black people were not compelled to speak up or speak out about major happenings locally, nationally, or worldwide. His silence would continue for his entire life.

For Dad, being a silent leader meant being contented with life. He was able to live and enjoy the freedom of his time. He was always positive and at peace. Many simple things were fulfilling to him, such as mowing the lawn and appreciating how it looked. This was very satisfying. Many of his children learned to appreciate this type of simple satisfaction.

The Vietnam War was a trying time for Dad and Mom. Two of their sons were in the military. One served in the Army and the other served in the Navy.

Some years prior to my brothers serving time in the military, we had a cousin who was young and in the Marines. He was killed in the Vietnam War. His remains were shipped back to Louisiana and a closed casket funeral was held. I was a young boy at that time. I went to the church to attend the funeral, but stayed in the car, as I was afraid. It was a very sad occasion.

I believe this weighed heavily on Dad and Mom, as two of their sons were sent to Vietnam. Questions in my parents' minds may have included: *Would they come home safely? Would they be shot or killed?* Even though I was growing up around my parents when this was going on, they never spoke of any of this in my presence or within earshot of me.

There was much joy and warmth of heart when they received a letter from my brothers. Dad and Mom for that moment knew their sons were alive.

Dad did not place his unfulfilled dreams and hopes on his children. He allowed each of us to decide our life's journey.

I wonder if Dad was afraid of putting high-achieving goals before us, based upon us living in the South under racial segregation. I never asked him about his feelings on this matter.

Dad never spoke of seeking a job promotion or pursuing a certain amount of income. He never placed emphasis on acquiring much materially.

His children followed this lead; for we, too, rarely spoke of job promotions and reaching for certain income amounts. This is an area where Dad's silent leadership needed to be challenged, as we lost our opportunity to encourage one another.

I have a sister-in-law who is white. When we would gather together for vacations, she frequently spoke of her pursuit of a promotion. She obtained the promotions she sought.

I always felt we did not have enough confidence to let one another know we wanted a certain job, and stayed silent out of fear of failure. We could silently desire, but not acquire. In this respect, I feel that silent leadership hurts.

As each of us children lived life in adulthood, we would frequently and unassumingly comment about things we valued thanks to observing Dad in his life.

My brother Albany once said he felt that his family (Dad, Mom, sisters and brothers) would never willingly lead him astray. He said this in the Acknowledgments of his 1994 book, *Crippled Pockets.* We often spoke of how Dad would handle his responsibilities without being prodded, pushed, or impelled. He saw what needed to be done and took action.

We all appreciated Dad being self-sufficient. This rubbed off on his children, for the most part. My older sister at one time needed some assistance, which our parents gladly provided.

As a silent leader, Dad helped raise us six children to be contributors to society. We became steady workers, husbands, and wives, and all but one became a parent.

For those of us who became parents, we, like Dad, did not place our unfulfilled dreams and hopes on our children. We, however, have been able to help our children achieve some of their dreams and hopes. I am very pleased that one of my children graduated from the same university as me. My other child graduated from a different university. This, too, is pleasing.

As a silent leader, Dad led his family through a difficult time period in human history (legal segregation). Each of us received enough stability, insight, and foresightedness to live as decent people. We lived with little fear of being killed, injured, or imprisoned during racial segregation.

Chapter 8 — Legacy

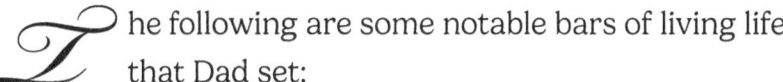

*T*he following are some notable bars of living life
that Dad set:

· He lived for 98 years, 11 months and 19 days.

· He lived in the same house for 54 years.

· He was married to Mom for 44 years.

· He was married to his second wife Doris for 30 years.
His total married time was 74 years.

· He owned his house and had no mortgage.

· He drove from age 18 to roughly 95 for a total of 77 years.

· He worked to earn income for 47 years.

· He was retired for nearly 34 years.

· Between his pension and Social Security, his total retirement
income was around $400,000, give or take some.

· He died without being in debt.

· He left an inheritance.

Dad became a world statistic by living to be 98 years,
11 months, 19 days old. He outlived the average age for

Black people, Black males, white people and all other races of people in the World.

Dad always had a positive attitude. When asked, "How are things going?" his reply was, "Everything is fine." He stayed calm almost all the time.

Dad was a leader, yet I do not believe he ever thought of himself as a leader. He always led by example. He developed good habits and applied them continuously. At the family reunion, he was recognized as the oldest person in the family. Dad cherished that blessing. When he died, he became the longest-living man in our family.

Dad almost lived a full century! He thought he was going to live to be 100 years old. He was healthy up until the near end of his life. He needed few prescription medicines during his final year of life.

Dad did not compare his children with one another. Nor did he compare us to himself. We were not in his shadow (except for my brother Albany having the same first name as Dad) and did not have to follow in his footsteps. He made sure each of us could receive our full opportunity to build our own lives.

Dad did not amass many titles to describe who he was; however, there was one title that he was proud to have and enjoy—Treasurer at church. As I said earlier, he merely collected the donations and deposited them in the bank. This meant that he was trusted and honest. His older brother had this honor before my dad, and he was honored to take up that torch.

Dad held the titles of dad, husband, uncle, employee, deacon, son, retiree, widower, granddad, great-granddad and great-great-granddad.

Dad left us a very bright light that is shining fully. The light is energized by his family. As we are motivated by his example, his light keeps burning brightly for each of us.

This book is a result of his light. He was blessed with much.

My father's greatest legacy is his family, and he was very happy to host our family every year during summer vacation.

"When the kids were little," Sheila recalled, "my sister-in-law Pat had two kids; we had two kids; and Albert and his wife had two kids. All three families stayed in a three-bedroom house with one bathroom. The kids took baths together, and somehow, we managed. It didn't seem difficult. The den had a couch that was a sofa bed, so we had four sleeping areas."

Sheila added, "We would visit for days without having disturbances or fighting or getting upset with one another. It was just joy."

A good portion of this joy, Sheila recalls, happened in our tradition of "The Circle." In the morning and afternoon, we put dozens of chairs in a semi-circle, so that some people could sit on the carport, while others sat in the yard. Dad painted these sturdy lawn chairs different colors, including white, green and black. The chairs were very comfortable, never wore out, and didn't rust.

Albany would be leading the pack as we talked about any and everything.

Sheila remembers how Dad would be in the mix, listening, and when he got an opportunity, he would chime in with what he had to say. Mostly he was overjoyed to have his adult kids all together, along with his grandchildren, and all of us being at peace with no drama.

"He is on Cloud Nine," Mom and Doris would say.

Nobody went hungry at these events. Our meals were planned and organized, and the prepared food would be in the kitchen, where everyone would pick up a paper plate and help themselves to each item. Then we would take our plates outside, get something to drink, and sit out there and enjoy the family.

We would spend hours talking, laughing, telling stories, and eating.

"You haven't had watermelon and cantaloupe and grapes until you've had it down there," Sheila said. "Louisiana has such good fruit."

We always had pop, water, and frozen drinks for the kids in coolers galore on the carport. We also had beer for the adults. The Circle brought together young and old, including at times, Dad's sisters and his brother, Uncle Buddy. It was beautiful to see the different generations interacting for this happy experience.

"That circle was so special," Sheila recalled, "and we had such a good time. The older kids who are now in their forties still talk about that circle."

When we visited with our families, we'd all be in the yard visiting and my dad and mom just had pride written all over their faces. They were overjoyed to have those social gatherings where they could see that us kids and our families were all doing well.

Our kids, Jeremy and Jerran, have happy memories of those trips.

"I was super excited to go down there," said Jeremy, who is 44 and is a Senior Departmental Analyst for the State of Michigan Licensing and Regulatory Affairs. "We went for like a week. It was really fun. I have fun memories of playing hide-and-seek with my cousins. My cousins' name for Grandpa was Paw Paw."

Jerran, who is 38 and is an accountant in Claymont, Delaware, shares this happy memory: "I was excited to see the family and have fun and see my cousins. I was happy to be going."

Jeremy added that, "Most of the time, we drove. I think we flew twice when I was older."

Jerran remembers taking airplanes to our annual summer trip to Louisiana: "We always flew. I don't recall driving."

Jeremy said he does not remember my mom because she passed away when he was five years old. But he does remember my dad. Since Mom died when Sheila was pregnant with Jerran, our daughter never met my mom.

Jerran playfully recalls, "Mosquitoes in Louisiana loved me! I had a million mosquito bites. It looked like chicken pox! When I was younger, I didn't mind, because I was having fun."

Jeremy's recollection is that his grandfather was quiet and happy when surrounded by family.

"Grandpa didn't say a whole lot," Jeremy recalled. "He was really quiet. I remember we used to sit in a circle on their carport. He would sit off to the side and listen to everyone."

Jerran added, "I don't recall him being the center of the conversation. He just enjoyed his family. I think he was just happy knowing that the family was there."

Jeremy added that his grandfather was content in the heat.

"I never saw Grandpa in shorts," he said. "Ever. It could be 100 degrees and he's got jeans on with the cuff rolled up like there's a flood coming. He always wore a baseball hat and a button up shirt. My cousin bought him a Michigan hat and he wore it all the time. That was his outfit. The heat didn't bother him. The rest of us were dying!"

Jeremy said his grandfather was an excellent grill master. "When I was really little and Grandpa was younger, he used to grill. That was the best! I loved the ribs and chicken."

Jeremy also remembered that his grandfather used to smoke cigars, and that, "Grandpa chewed tobacco the whole time I knew him."

Jeremy said he only saw his grandfather get upset once. "When I was a kid, he had a green truck and we would slide down the window. Grandpa said, 'Hey, you guys can't do that!' That's the only time I remember him getting mad."

As the kids grew up, the families needed more space, so we all tried to stay at the same hotel. The kids could swim together, and we'd all meet back at the house.

Another family tradition was a family reunion every three years. Hundreds of people attended those events that were very well-organized by Cousin Willie, who was president of the family reunion committee.

Each reunion started on Friday night with a fish fry, where everyone got acquainted. On Saturday, we enjoyed a picnic with barbecue, games such as bingo and basketball, and introductions to new family members that, thanks to births and marriages, kept us meeting new people.

Our reunion programs featured an emcee and a dee-jay. Some people displayed talents. For example, Albany read a poem. One year, our grandson Amare treated us to a hip hop dance performance. Everyone was clapping and cheering, amazed by his talent. We also gave away prizes for winners of the bingo games.

On Sunday, some enjoyed a religious gathering at church. At the last reunion we attended in 2013, Dad was recognized as the oldest family member when he was 96. My Aunt Lola, at a prior reunion, was recognized as the oldest in the family. This recognition was received with honor by Dad and Aunt Lola.

One year, somebody created a design for the back of the family reunion t-shirts; it was a family tree, with families branching out from the tree with a road down the middle of the tree.

Each year, we looked forward to where the reunion would be held. One year, the reunion was in the large yard of Cousin Oscar Devers. He took people on a hayride going way back into the family property, which is on Devers Road in Greenwood, Louisiana.

Our family reunions inspired conversations about the history of the land, which my parents had never discussed. On that road, the family owned a lot of land. A lot of the families inherited land from there. Dad inherited some. He sold it to Oscar, our first cousin. Oscar purchased Dad's property, along with Aunt Daisy's and Aunt Lola's. Cousin Oscar is the only one in our family who has a house on Devers Road, which is paved. It was gravel when I was growing up. My parents never said anything about living on it.

It was such an honor when I was riding the school bus to elementary school and we passed Devers Road.

We have not had a family reunion since 2019, but our family cherishes them as part of the legacy that Dad and others created for all of us.

Chapter 9 — Saying "I Love You"

*D*ad provided well for his family. He always had a job to earn money during my upbringing. We always had plenty of food to eat. A house to live in. Clothes to wear. He provided spiritual nourishment by taking us to church every Sunday.

None in the family complained much, because we were at peace with what we had. We had our material needs met. Those who wanted to pursue learning music and playing an instrument were able to do so. As we came of age, most of us learned to drive. And when we were old enough, we were free to get a summer job and have some money in our pockets.

Yes, we had a very strong foundation of faith and family. But I never heard Dad or Mom say, "I love you," to each other. And as siblings, we did not say, "I love you," to each other while growing up. At the same time, while I was growing up, neither Dad nor Mom said, "I love you," to me.

Dad and Mom attended the weddings of four of their children. They were able to attend the births of two of their grandchildren. Family life brought many blessings to all of us. We learned how to be self-sufficient, how to help others, how to give of ourselves, and how to prepare for our own family. Dad and Mom were pleased with the husbands chosen by their daughters and the wives of their sons. Each son-in-law and daughter-in-law became an integral part of the family. They made the new family members feel welcome and at ease. Each new member called my parents Dad and Mom. My oldest brother was not married while Mom was alive.

I married Sheila on July 26, 1975. Dad, Mom, Aunt Viola, and Aunt Lola came from Shreveport to attend our wedding in a Baptist church in Jackson, Michigan. All my siblings, except for Raymond, were among the 200 guests. Albany was my best man and Pat was a bridesmaid.

After being introduced by one of my cousins, Sheila and I started dating in 1974.

"I saw that Vernon was a person that was determined to do what he planned to do," said Sheila, who was living in East Lansing. "I saw that he was self-sufficient. He had his own apartment. We never lived together before we married. He loved to save money. He would plan what he needed for school and take care of that. He didn't like to drink. I never heard him use profanity. We would go to the movies and go out dancing, then started seeing each other every day. Even though my parents had divorced, I had always said, 'To the best of my ability, I want to stay married.' And as I got to know Vernon, I thought, *This is a person I could stay married to.*"

That proved to be true, as we are celebrating 48 years of marriage this year.

Unfortunately, two of my siblings divorced their mates and this brought sadness to the family. Divorce did occur, yet it did not end love for such ones. That's family!

Dad carried his emotional pain well. After military service, my older brother Albany remained away from the family for many years. We all wanted to see him and hear from him. During his absence, Dad's emotional pain was kept silent. We would often ask one another, "Have you talked to Albany?"

After I had been married for years and Dad was older, he said, "I love you, son."

I do not recall if Mom ever said to me, "I love you."

I never said to either of my parents, "I love you." I have never said, "I love you," to my siblings.

Even though I grew up in a family where we never said, "I love you," to one another, our family was and is still full of love. Love was lived and shown.

In 1985, Dad lost Mom to death. Dad was saddened by Mom's death. It was long in coming, as she suffered from diabetes and its complications.

I lived more than 1,000 miles away from Dad and Mom. My sister Sylvia, who lived within 20 miles of Dad and Mom, informed my siblings and me of Mom's death. My immediate family and I flew to Shreveport, Louisiana the next day. The night before was an ice storm in Michigan. It was slow traveling from the Lansing suburb of Haslett to Detroit for the flight.

Dad was very pleased to receive each of his children, as most of us lived out of state. We began to arrive one family at a time. During this time, Dad did not have time to be alone. The neighbors and family surrounded him immediately.

For a short period of time after Mom's death, Dad drank much alcohol to ease the loss. My sister Sylvia and her family moved onto my parents' property to comfort Dad.

In time, Dad adjusted to a new normal after Mom's death and he went on to marry another woman, Doris, a widow with three adult children. She was a very nice lady who was well-established in Dallas, and moved to Shreveport and enjoyed 30 years of marriage with Dad; she died one year after he passed.

Dad was pleased and happy with both of his wives. His wives were also pleased and happy with him and the life they shared together.

Dad said "I do" twice—once to Mom and once to his second wife Doris. Both "I do's" ended in death. First, death of Mom, and second, his death to Doris. For each marriage, his "I do's" included his willing care, forgiveness, hope, peace, sacrifice and love. He succeeded in two marriages. His wives were happy.

Sadly, Dad experienced the deaths of two of my three

siblings who have passed. Sylvia died on August 13, 2013, after a long battle with diabetes and its complications.

Dad tried to hide his feelings of pain. The next year, Dad lost another child to death. This time, it was our brother Raymond. He, too, suffered a long time with diabetes and its complications, and died on April 4, 2014.

When Sylvia died, Dad was 96 years old, and 97 when Raymond died. Dad never talked to me about these deaths.

Dad had already passed when Patricia, who had diabetes and pancreatic cancer, died on March 16, 2018. When her health deteriorated and she was in the hospital in Lansing, we visited her every day. Surrounded by Pat's husband, Leon, my wife Sheila, my brother Albany, and Pat's daughters, LaTrish and Charmaine, I witnessed my sister as she took her last breath.

My brother Albany says, "I love you," on a regular basis to me and many others. He has done this for years. Even though I am older, I still find it hard for those words to roll off my tongue. It is in my heart and I try to show it, rather than say it.

I believe it is best to both say, "I love you," to people and show it. I love my wife, children, family, siblings, grandson, nieces, nephews, friends, spiritual brothers and sisters, and any whom I may have left out.

In 2015, it was Dad's turn to draw closer to his death. He spent a considerable amount of time in bed. He was cold almost all the time.

Albert and his wife Earsel, who lived about five miles away, started caring for Dad and Doris when he was about 96.

I received a call from Cousin Oscar, who said, "You guys need to get here. Uncle D can't take care of himself anymore."

I called Albany and said, "I'll catch a flight," and he said, "No, I'll go." He stayed a few weeks.

Since Dad and Doris wanted to stay in the house, Albert and Earsel took care of Dad and Doris by taking them meals and cleaning the house, until that wasn't working anymore.

Dad entered a nursing home for three months before he died. He got sick in the nursing home, and was transferred to the VA hospital. During this time, Doris stayed in the house until her children came to take her back to Dallas where they could care for her. She was 88 when she died, 10 years younger than Dad.

Albany, the oldest son, had traveled from Chicago to Shreveport to be with both Dad and Albert. Albert, the fourth child, was in the VA hospital for cancer surgery when Dad was brought from the nursing home to the same VA hospital for care. After some days, Albany left and returned to Chicago. Albert was released from the hospital the morning of January 20th, and we received a phone call later in the day that Dad died the afternoon of January 20, 2016. Sadly, Dad passed away alone, without any family members by his side.

Dad's funeral was not as organized as I had wanted.

The VA paid for part of Dad's military funeral that drew less than 50 people to Northwestern Veterans Cemetery, where a flag was folded over his coffin and handed to the oldest son, Albany, during the graveside ceremony. I was there with Sheila and our grown kids, Jeremy and Jerran, Albany, Pat and Pat's children.

"The funeral was sad," Jeremy said. "While I was growing up, my grandpa was always fine. Then you start to see when somebody gets older, you see things happen that didn't happen before, that was weird. It's like you know it's coming, but you don't want it to. He passed away two weeks before his 99th birthday. We were like, 'Man, it would've been so cool if he could have made it to 100.'"

Jerran remembered the funeral being emotional, with many relatives crying.

"That was a hard situation," she said. "There's not too many times that I've seen my dad cry. My grandpa was 98, but still, you never really prepare yourself for it."

We visit Dad's grave almost every time we return to Shreveport.

Lesson learned: Do not wait to be with your loved ones. We cannot change the last days of Dad's life. Dad was a happy, positive man. He never complained. This is our ongoing example as we live our lives.

Conclusion

I am honored to write about my dad, to describe the things he did and showed to others. As an obedient respectful child, then as an adult, he held onto those qualities and passed them on to his children.

Dad used his educational attainment, limited as it was, to forge a living for himself, a wife and six children. This all took place in a segregated part of the U.S.A., which afforded limited opportunities for Colored people, as we were called during much of his early life.

One of Dad's strengths was to maintain a positive mental attitude, no matter what. Well, I drew and drew and am still drawing upon Dad's strengths. It is my hope that all readers of this book find many teaching points that you, too, can draw upon, talk to others about, and see some of life's history through my dad's life.

There are many stories and ways of describing living in the South from 1917 to 2016; this writing is just one. More than half of Dad's life was lived in segregation. Only a small part of my life was lived in segregation. It was difficult to see the bright lights, yet Dad saw them and kept them before him as he walked through life.

I hope educators will have many classroom discussions with students for years, even decades, of how this one individual lived. I also hope many families will have many good conversations about how Dad lived.

As of this writing, I can only recall meeting one other man of Dad's age. To live 98 years, 11 months, and 19 days provided Dad with nine decades-plus of memories. I am thankful for the time we shared, events we experienced, and our joys. My dad's legacy is alive in me. I hope the readers of this book can find some points of interest and appreciate one man who lived a long, happy life.

One last story from me. If not for this blessing, Dad's life and experiences that are talked about in this book would have been different, to say the least. One summer night, Dad came alone to Waskom, Texas, to cousins' Will and Roberta Ragland's house to pick me up. I was very young, perhaps five years old. We all heard the chickens making noise. Cousin Will, an older man, gave Dad a flashlight and a rifle to use. Dad carefully went to the chicken coop. There were no lights outside. They did not have any electricity. Dad saw a snake in one of the chicken beds. He pointed and fired the rifle. It had not been cleaned or used in a long time. It exploded and hit Dad in one of his eyes. Blood was flowing and we were shocked and scared. Cousin Roberta stopped the bleeding. After getting some composure, Dad and I got in the vehicle and he drove as best as he could. By the way, it was raining very hard. We made it safely home in Louisiana.

I do not remember how Dad was helped after getting home. However, he recovered and had no eye or vision damage. He did not miss any work time. What a blessing!

A NOTE FROM SHEILA DEVERS, WIFE OF VERNON DEVERS

For 40 years, I knew my father-in-law as "D." This is the name most people used (other than immediate family members) when talking to Dad. I personally called him Dad. I met my future father-in-law and mother-in-law a day or two before our wedding. They traveled from Louisiana, along with a couple of Vernon's aunts, to help us celebrate our special day! I had spoken to them on the phone, thus knew they were pleasant people; however, I was still a bit nervous! I was marrying their son, their youngest child! I had no reason to be nervous, however, because they were delightful people. They made me feel relaxed and welcomed me to the family.

The next 40 years were filled with growing closer to my in-laws. We would travel down to Louisiana from Michigan pretty much every summer to visit. We were always excited and looked forward to the trip.

In the early years, we would drive, and then later we would fly and rent a vehicle there. The whole experience was a joyful summer, despite the heat, visiting relatives!

In time, two of Vernon's siblings, including us, had children. Some summers when the kids were all young, there would be as many as 14 persons staying at my in-laws' home, which had three bedrooms, a den with a sofa bed, and one bathroom.

My mother-in-law said with love, "Don't worry, it will all work out."

Wow, did it ever! They were such gracious hosts! Dad and Mom never complained and were content just to have all of us there and show hospitality to their family! Dad would sit on the carport in one of his newly-painted patio armchairs—white one year, black another and light green another—chewing his tobacco with his legs crossed and just glowing as he watched his grandchildren playing, getting into mischief by trying to climb the trees, and taking note of various conversations, all with a satisfied, fulfilled countenance.

One year when our son Jeremy was five months old, we traveled to Shreveport by airplane. In 1979, one could wait right inside the airport and greet arriving passengers as they deplaned. When my mother-in-law-saw us, without greeting anyone, she held out her arms to grab Jeremy. She was thrilled to see and meet her new grandson. Seeing her embrace him absolutely warmed my heart and endeared her to me even more. Our son arrived in a Michigan State University jogging suit which my own mother had given to him. We returned home to Michigan with a Dallas Cowboys jogging suit my mother-in-law purchased for him. What a chuckle that gave me!

When we were in Louisiana, there was what we called "The Circle," which we formed on the adjacent lot which my in-laws owned. Everyone would grab a chair, find their location and form a circle—thus the name. Dad was in the center of us! Many colorful conversations ensued and folks would share experiences. Of course, the conversations always turned to food, which called for figuring out what we were going to have for dinner and who was going to pick it up! Dad and the rest of us made sure there were always plenty of cool drinks in the coolers, enough for the family and anyone who stopped by. What a host! Needless to say, good times were had by all. I think my father-in-law truly enjoyed these times! I, and many of us, fondly remember "The Circle!"

In 1985, the year our daughter was born, my mother-in-law, Luella died. What an incredibly sad time this was for me and the family. My mother-in-law was a gem, and I mean a *gem* of a lady. She was always pleasant, industrious, supportive of her husband, and so encouraging to me and Vernon. She never spoke a cross word. Plus, I was reflecting that our daughter, who was born four months later, along with another grandson born at the same time, wouldn't have the privilege to meet and love their grandmother as I loved her!

Mom had a nice funeral. All in the family were concerned about Dad, worrying, *How will he handle not having Mom and will he be okay?* For several days after, we all comforted Dad and each other! Before we left to return to our homes, my sister-in-law, Sylvia, informed us that she and her family would be moving their mobile home onto Dad's property, the adjacent lot, so he would not be alone. How do you spell R E L I E F! We were all so pleased for their helpfulness and love!

Dad met and married a wonderful widow named Doris. The two of them were happily married for nearly 31 years. Each year as we visited them, Doris would say, "Look, D has his chest poked out. He is so happy having all of you visit!"

It was difficult to see Dad getting older and slowing down; he was always energetic, barbequing in the backyard, mowing the yard, driving his green truck and puttering around the house. However, the time comes when we all grow older, so we accept it with grace. I don't think he appreciated being told, "It's time to stop driving, though, because he liked that independence that enabled him to go to the store each morning!

For my 40 years of knowing Dad and all of us visiting together, there were never any problems. We enjoyed being with one another. Again, Dad was always a gracious host and welcoming! It was a sad day in January 2016 when we lost him! Things changed, as they often do when both parents are deceased. Louisiana wasn't the same, our ties were loosening... all the laughter, talking and visiting with one another at the house went away. The house was sold, no more of "The Circle!"

Of course, the family still keeps in touch with one

another, but it's not the same as when Dad and the house were there!

My father-in-law was a gentle, mild-mannered man and I count it as an absolute privilege and pleasure to have known him.

About the Author

Vernon Jerome Devers was born on October 28, 1952, in Shreveport, Louisiana. The last of six children born to Albany and Luella Devers, he was raised from infancy with Bible-based values and principles as his guiding light. He endeavored to be a good son and endeavors to be a good brother, good uncle, good husband, good dad, good granddad, good cousin and good friend.

He resides in Okemos, Michigan with his wife of 48 years, Sheila Devers. Together they raised two responsible children. After receiving a Bachelor of Arts degree from Michigan State University, he earned an Associate's in Underwriting degree from the Insurance Institute of America. He then happily spent 36 years in service to Auto-Owners Insurance Company.

ENDNOTES

[1] https://www.greenwoodla.org/about-us.html

[2] https://en.wikipedia.org/wiki/Greenwood,_Louisiana

www.ingramcontent.com/pod-product-compliance
Lightning Source LLC
Chambersburg PA
CBHW021652120626
46545CB00002B/829